Word Strategies

Building a Strong Vocabulary
High-Beginning Level

Janet Giannotti
Northern Virginia Community College

New Readers Press

Word Strategies, High-Beginning Level
ISBN 978-1-56420-522-3

Copyright © 2007 New Readers Press
New Readers Press
Division of ProLiteracy Worldwide
1320 Jamesville Avenue, Syracuse, New York 13210
www.newreaderspress.com

Printed in the United States of America
9 8 7 6 5 4 3 2 1

All proceeds from the sale of New Readers Press materials
support literacy programs in the United States and worldwide.

Developmental Editor: Paula L. Schlusberg
Creative Director: Andrea Woodbury
Illustrations: Linda Tiff
Production Specialist: Jeffrey R. Smith

Contents

To the Student

Sometimes you say, "I know that word."

What does this mean? When you know a word, you know a lot about the word, and you can do a lot with it.

- You can read the dictionary definition of the word and understand it.
- If the word has an abbreviation or shortened form, you know it.
- If the word is part of an initialization, you know the initialization. Initializations are short forms of two or more words, using the first letters of the words.
- You can add a prefix to the word to change the meaning.
- You can add a suffix to the word to change the part of speech.
- You understand the spelling changes that occur when you add a suffix to the word.
- You can think of one or more close synonyms for the word.
- You can think of an antonym, or opposite, for the word.
- You can use the word in a collocation. Collocations are fixed phrases of two or more words that are used together in a particular order.
- You understand fine points of meaning and grammar so that you do not confuse the word with similar words.
- You know how the word works in the context of other words.
- You know what part of speech the word is, even if you are not sure of the exact meaning.
- You can select the appropriate definition of the word from a list in your dictionary, even if the word has several definitions.

As you can see, there are many ways you can know a word. You can know a word to different degrees as well. You can simply guess the general meaning of the word. You can look up a word quickly in a dictionary. You can change a word with prefixes and suffixes. Or, you can quickly bring to mind a synonym or an antonym.

Word Strategies will help you know words better. The two-book set allows you to get to know hundreds of words in all of the ways outlined above. The first book presents words from your everyday life, including words about learning a language, shopping, job hunting, and TV. The second book presents more specialized words on subjects like the federal government, crime, computers, and health care. By completing both books, you can improve your vocabulary for school, work, and your everyday life.

To the Teacher

Welcome to *Word Strategies.* This two-book set has been designed to increase your students' word knowledge in all the ways outlined in "To the Student."

Each contextualized lesson begins with a short **reading** that presents the first dozen words of the lesson. In the first book (high-beginning level), the readings alternate between dialogs and simple narratives. In the second book (low-intermediate level), narratives alternate with expository readings. In the readings and throughout the exercises, students should be encouraged to use their learner's dictionaries to look up unfamiliar words that are not overtly taught in the lesson.

After the reading, students are asked to match the words with dictionary **definitions.** This should be an easy exercise that familiarizes students with the wording of dictionary definitions. The definitions presented here fit the way a word is used in the lesson's reading exactly. Later in the lesson, students work with their dictionaries to choose the best definition of a word in context.

The next part of the lesson presents students with **initializations** or **abbreviations** associated with the context. In some lessons, you may wish to extend this section with realia. For example, newspaper advertisements for cars, computers, or banks and financial services may contain initializations or abbreviations. Supermarket ads and weather reports can also be used. Or, students can search the Internet or use a map for weather, airport, and state abbreviations.

The first book then presents a section on **compound words.** Students who struggle with vocabulary may not realize that longer words are often made up of smaller, well-known words. Studying compounds can increase vocabulary and help students with their spelling.

Following that, both books have a section called **word building.** This section teaches students **prefixes** that change the meanings of words and **suffixes** that change the forms of words. This section also deals with spelling changes that occur when suffixes are added.

Each lesson then has an exercise on either **synonyms** or **antonyms.** Complete knowledge of a word allows students to access both synonyms and antonyms quickly. Some of the pairs in these exercises may seem easy; the purpose of this section is not specifically to build knowledge of pairs of words as much as it is to build facility in retrieving synonyms or antonyms.

After that, students focus on several **collocations,** or fixed phrases, associated with the context. For example, they learn that in American English, we attend a concert in a concert *hall,* but we attend a movie in a movie *theater.* The words in collocations always occur in a set order, so students learn to say we will have the picnic *rain or shine,* not *shine or rain.* They also work with collocations that involve common verbs like *pay* or *take,* in combination with prepositions.

The next section deals with **confusing words.** In this section, students should discuss fine distinctions between pairs of words. Some words in this section are content words that are similar in meaning, such as *teach* and *learn,* or *see* and *watch.*

Others are function words or phrases, like *a few* and *a little,* or *very* and *too.*

After that, students learn about context. Even the most comprehensive vocabulary program can't teach every word students will come across. Therefore, they need to practice relying on context. The first book asks students to rely on the most typical type of **context clue,** which is often identified as *general description.* While this section may feel like vocabulary review to students, these exercises train them to look at rich context as they read sentences and to choose words to complete those sentences. In the second book, students are introduced to other types of context clues, including noticing definitions or defining examples after dashes, and finding signals that indicate whether pairs of words are synonyms or antonyms.

The last two sections get students ready to use their dictionaries efficiently to look up words. When a student encounters an unfamiliar word, the first step is to identify the **part of speech**—the way the word is working in that particular context. This can be a challenge in English, since many words serve double duty as nouns and verbs, as verbs and gerunds, as verbs and adjectives, and as adjectives and adverbs. Controlled exercises help students become more confident in recognizing parts of speech.

Finally, students are asked to look up words in a **dictionary.** Words in this exercise have been chosen because they have multiple meanings. It is the students' job to choose the best definition for the way the word is used in context. This is not a simple exercise and may best be done in class with large dictionaries that you provide, or with an online dictionary.

Each lesson ends with two review exercises: a **crossword puzzle** and a **vocabulary in context** exercise. These two activities recycle many of the words in the lesson.

An answer key appears at the end of each text.

Language

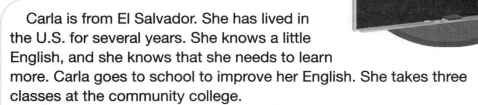

In this lesson, you will work with words that help us talk about language. Read this story about Carla's English class.

Carla is from El Salvador. She has lived in the U.S. for several years. She knows a little English, and she knows that she needs to learn more. Carla goes to school to improve her English. She takes three classes at the community college.

Carla has a grammar class on Monday nights. She learns about parts of speech. She studies about **nouns** and **pronouns**. She studies about **verbs**. She learns about **adjectives** and **adverbs**. She practices using articles and prepositions. Carla thinks grammar is easy. She likes to memorize rules and forms.

Carla studies vocabulary on Tuesdays and Thursdays. She learns new words. She finds the words in her dictionary. She learns the forms of the new words. For example, when Carla learns a noun, she learns the **plural** form. When Carla learns a verb, she learns the past tense form. She also memorizes **collocations**. Carla likes learning **compound words**, too. She thinks that is a good way to learn longer words and expand her vocabulary.

On Wednesdays, Carla has her oral communication class. She improves her pronunciation in that class. She works on the sounds of English. Carla has trouble with English **vowels**. Some **consonants** are difficult, too. Carla also practices the **stress** and **intonation** of English. The teacher records Carla's voice. Carla doesn't like to hear her own voice, but she is happy that her pronunciation is improving.

It's hard to go to school four nights a week, but Carla thinks she gets a lot out of the classes.

Definitions

Write each word or phrase next to its definition.

> | | | | |
> |---|---|---|---|
> | adjective | compound word | noun | stress |
> | adverb | consonant | plural | verb |
> | collocation | intonation | pronoun | vowel |

_____ 1. a word that names or represents a person, place, thing, quality, action, or idea

_____ 2. a word that is made up of two or more words written as one word with a special meaning that comes from the combination of words

_____ 3. having to do with the form of a noun that shows that there is more than one

_____ 4. a word that describes or adds to the meaning of a verb, adjective, adverb, or whole sentence

_____ 5. a speech sound made by stopping or restricting the flow of air through the mouth with the tongue, teeth, or lips

_____ 6. a speech sound made by letting breath flow out without closing any part of your mouth

_____ 7. a word that is used in place of a noun or noun phrase

_____ 8. the way in which the level and pitch of your voice changes when you are speaking

_____ 9. the emphasis placed on a syllable that makes it louder and longer than other syllables

_____ 10. a word that expresses an action, an experience, or a state of being

_____ 11. a word that describes a noun or pronoun

_____ 12. a particular combination of two or more words that are often used together

Abbreviations

Match each abbreviation with the word that it represents.

> Many words associated with grammar and vocabulary are abbreviated. When you read an abbreviation, you say the whole word. For example, when you read *adj.* you say *adjective.*

_____ 1. adj.   a. noun

_____ 2. adv.   b. preposition

_____ 3. art.   c. adverb

_____ 4. n.   d. pronoun

_____ 5. pl.   e. adjective

_____ 6. prep.   f. plural

_____ 7. pron.   g. verb

_____ 8. v.   h. article

Exercise 3

Compound Words

Choose a word from each box. Combine the words into a compound word. Write the new word on the line.

> Compound words are words made up of two or more words. Each is written as one word and has a special meaning that comes from the combination of words.

class	day	text	week
book	him	them	with

book	mates	self	shelf
end	out	selves	time

1. She works in the _____, not at night.

2. He does his homework by _____. He doesn't get help.

3. Carla enjoys talking with her _____ on her break at school.

4. The plural of *itself* is _____.

5. Carla loves vocabulary, so she has a dictionary on her _____.

6. Her classes are not on the _____; they are Monday through Thursday.

7. Carla had to buy her _____ in the bookstore.

8. Now she can read the newspaper _____ using her dictionary.

Prefix

Discuss the meanings of the words in the box. Then choose a word from the box and write it on the line.

bicentennial	**bilingual**	**biplane**
bicycle	**bimonthly**	**biweekly**

1. If Carla has a _____ test, she has it either twice a week or once every two weeks.

2. Since Carla speaks two languages, we say that she is _____.

3. A _____ has two wheels.

4. If Carla has a _____ assignment, it can be due either twice a month or once every two months.

5. Carla read a story about a _____, an airplane with two wings.

6. The class read about a _____ celebration, which was like a 200th birthday.

Suffix

When you add *–able* to a verb, you create an adjective that means *capable of.* Example: drink + able = drinkable

Fill in the adjective form of the verb in parentheses.

1. (accept)   Carla's pronunciation was _____.

2. (count)   The grammar class was about _____ nouns.

3. (enjoy)   Carla says the classes are _____.

4. (comfort)   The chairs are not _____.

5. (break)   Don't put anything _____ in your bag.

6. (depend)   Her classmates are very _____.

7. (disagree)   Carla hated classes with her _____ teacher.

8. (predict)   The questions on the test were _____.

Synonyms

Choose a word from the box which means about the same as each underlined
word or phrase. Write the word on the line.

courses	grammar	improve	syntax
difficulty	idioms	oral	vocabulary

1. Carla takes a _____ class. She studies the <u>structure</u> of English.

2. English _____ is easy, but in some languages <u>word order</u> is hard.

3. Carla learns new <u>words</u> in her _____ class.

4. She learns new _____, like the <u>expression</u>, *piece of cake.*

5. She wanted to _____ her English, and she knows it's <u>getting better</u>.

6. She took three <u>classes</u> this term. Next time she's taking just two _____.

7. She has trouble <u>speaking</u>, so she took _____ communication.

8. Carla has no <u>trouble</u> reading, but she has some _____ speaking.

Collocations

Many collocations use *as . . . as* to add emphasis to an adjective.

Choose a word from the box and write it on
the line to complete each collocation.

bear	hills	pin
gold	pie	rock

1. She though the test was as easy as _____.

2. The classroom was as neat as a _____.

3. The uncomfortable chair was as hard as a _____.

4. That's an old joke. It's as old as the _____.

5. Her children were as good as _____.

6. By lunch time, I was as hungry as a _____.

Confusing Words

Write *for* or *since* on the line.

> *For* and *since* are both used with present perfect verbs to tell about the time of an action. *For* tells how long an action or state has continued over time. *Since* tells when an action or state began.

1. Carla has lived here _____ several years.

2. She has taken classes _____ last year.

3. She has taken classes _____ one year.

4. Carla has been in a grammar class _____ three months.

5. She has been in a pronunciation class _____ January.

6. We have been in class _____ 6:30.

7. I've been in this chair _____ an hour.

8. We have been memorizing verbs _____ the break ended.

Circle the words that best complete each sentence.

> *A little* and *a few* are both quantifiers. Use *a little* before a noncount noun. Noncount nouns are never plural. Use *a few* before a countable noun that is plural.

9. I am having (a little/a few) trouble memorizing verbs.

10. I looked up (a little/a few) words in my dictionary.

11. I think we are having (a little/a few) tests this month.

12. The teacher wrote (a little/a few) sentences on the board.

13. The oral communication teacher only gives (a little/a few) homework.

14. The grammar teacher assigns (a little/a few) writing in her class.

15. We had to memorize (a little/a few) prefixes.

16. I want to learn (a little/a few) new idioms.

Context Clues

Choose a word from below each line
and write it on the line.

It is often possible to guess a missing word from the context of a sentence. When you rely on context, you use what you know about the other words in the sentence to help you guess the word.

1. We know that if you want a plural form, you add –s to a noun, and that if you want to
   change plural to _____, you take off the –s.
   singular / comparative / past

2. Carla loves learning about the structures of English in her grammar class, and she also
   loves learning new words and collocations in her _____ class.
   pronunciation / grammar / vocabulary

3. An adverb can describe a verb, an adjective, another adverb, or a whole sentence, but an
   _____ just describes a noun.
   article / adjective / adverb

4. When we study _____, we learn how to use commas, periods,
   vocabulary / articles / punctuation
   and quotation marks.

5. In her pronunciation class, Carla works on the sounds, _____,
   stress / grammar / vocabulary
   and intonation of English.

6. A lot of people have trouble learning the _____ a and the.
   articles / prepositions / syllables

7. She had problems with her _____, so her word order was
   intonation / syntax / consonants
   always wrong.

8. We have to learn a lot of _____, like I, me, mine, and myself.
   nouns / syllables / pronouns

Parts of Speech

Identify the underlined words. Write *N*
on the line if the word is a noun, and
write *V* if it is a verb.

> Many common vocabulary words can work either as
> nouns or verbs. Look for a noun after *the.* Look for a
> verb after *to.*

_____ 1. I did the <u>exercise</u> this morning.

_____ 2. We finished all of the <u>work</u>.

_____ 3. If you want to get better, you need to <u>exercise</u>.

_____ 4. In order to <u>form</u> the past tense, add *–ed.*

_____ 5. Syntax is usually defined as the <u>study</u> of word order.

_____ 6. I don't like to <u>work</u> at night.

_____ 7. We had to memorize the <u>form</u> and the meaning.

_____ 8. If you want to learn, you need to <u>study</u>.

Dictionary

Identify the part of speech of each underlined word. Write *N* or *V* on
the line. Then look up the word in your dictionary. Choose and write
the best definition.

_____ 1. They learned about <u>stress</u> and intonation in the pronunciation class.

definition: _____

_____ 2. We asked the teacher to explain some <u>expressions</u> in the lesson on idioms.

definition: _____

_____ 3. The reading class looked at an <u>article</u> from the newspaper.

definition: _____

_____ 4. She wants to be able to <u>express</u> herself better in English.

definition: _____

_____ 5. Put a comma after the <u>clause</u> in that sentence.

definition: _____

Crossword Puzzle

Fill in the puzzle with words from the box.

art.	bookshelf	countable	little	plural	syntax
bilingual	collocation	difficulty	oral	prep.	vowel
bimonthly	compound	few	pie	rock	weekend

ACROSS

4. The word _____ describes two or more words that frequently appear together.
6. _____ is the abbreviation for *preposition*.
7. Many people get paid _____.
9. You can use *a few* before a _____ noun that is plural.
12. She works on speaking in her _____ communication class.
13. If I think the test is not difficult, I say that it is as easy as _____.
14. _____ is the study of word order.
16. Many people have _____ with English spelling.
18. When you make a _____ sound, you don't close any part of your mouth.

DOWN

1. To make a noun _____, you frequently just add –*s*.
2. A _____ word is a word that is made up of two or more words.
3. A person who is _____ speaks two languages.
5. The abbreviation for *article* is _____.
8. Carla studied a _____ grammar back home.
10. She keeps her dictionary on her _____.
11. Most students don't have classes on the _____.
15. I complained that my chair was as hard as a _____.
17. Carla memorized a _____ new vocabulary words.

Vocabulary in Context
Choose a word from the box and write it on the line.

| consonant | intonation | stress | trouble | vowel |

Carla has _____ 1 with English pronunciation. She has difficulty with some
_____ 2 sounds, like *b* and *v.* She also has to work on some
_____ 3 sounds, including short *i* and short *e.* She also works on syllable
_____ 4 . And she knows that if she improves her _____ 5 , her
English will sound more natural.

| bicycle | biweekly | daytime | dependable | enjoyable |

Carla rides her _____ 6 twice a week. She never rides at night. She always rides
in the _____ 7 . Carla has an old bike, but it is very _____ 8 . It
never breaks. Carla thinks that her _____ 9 bike rides are very
_____ 10 .

| classmates | himself | idioms | textbook | without |

Carla and her _____ 11 love the _____ 12 that their grammar teacher
uses. They use it in class and at home. Their vocabulary teacher, on the other hand, likes to
teach _____ 13 a book. He makes up all the exercises by _____ 14 .
The students would rather learn _____ 15 and expressions from a book.

Television

In this lesson, you will work with words about TV. Read this conversation between Ed and Pete.

Ed: Did you watch that new **sitcom** on Channel 7 last night?

Pete: No. I really don't watch much TV.

Ed: Really? Do you even own a TV set?

Pete: Oh, yes, I own one. But I don't have **cable**. I can only watch what I can pick up with my **antenna**.

Ed: I watch so much TV that I can't imagine life without cable.

Pete: I really only watch the news. I watch both **local** and national news **broadcasts**. I like to keep up with news, sports, and weather. But after the news I turn the TV off.

Ed: You mean you don't watch sitcoms or **dramas?**

Pete: Nope. Usually, if it's not **live** TV, I don't watch it.

Ed: How about news magazines—those hour-long shows that investigate issues—or talk shows?

Pete: Once in a while I watch a news magazine, but I really don't like talk shows. I do like **documentaries,** however. But I only watch them on public television, since I don't like **commercials**.

Ed: I really like game shows.

Pete: I can't stand game shows! I also hate **soap operas**.

Ed: Well, I have to agree with you there. I don't like soap operas either. But many people think that TV both **informs** and **entertains**. I'm surprised you don't watch more.

Pete: I guess I'd rather be out doing things. Say, do you want to go to a ballgame later? I have an extra ticket!

Ed: No thanks. I think I'll just watch the game on TV.

Definitions
Write each word or phrase next to its definition.

> antenna   commercial   entertain   local
> broadcast   documentary   inform   sitcom
> cable   drama   live   soap opera

_____ 1. a TV program that gives facts about something or someone

_____ 2. a TV or radio program

_____ 3. a TV program, usually broadcast on weekday afternoons, that is about the daily lives of a group of people

_____ 4. a TV or radio advertisement, usually lasting from 30 seconds to one minute

_____ 5. a TV show, movie, or play that is serious rather than funny

_____ 6. to amuse or interest someone

_____ 7. a piece of equipment that is used for receiving TV or radio signals

_____ 8. to give someone facts and ideas, usually in a formal way

_____ 9. performed while people are watching rather than recorded for later broadcast

_____ 10. a funny, 30-minute TV program in which the same characters appear every week; a situation comedy

_____ 11. having to do with a particular place such as a city or a town

_____ 12. a system of broadcasting TV signals that uses wires rather than transmitting the signal through the air

Initializations

Match each initialization with the words that it represents.

Many TV networks and production companies are identified by sets of initials. You can explain these initializations with sentences using *stands for.*

_____ 1. NBC   a. Columbia Broadcasting System

_____ 2. ABC   b. Home Box Office

_____ 3. CBS   c. The Learning Channel

_____ 4. MTV   d. National Broadcasting Company

_____ 5. PBS   e. Public Broadcasting Service

_____ 6. TLC   f. American Broadcasting Company

_____ 7. CNN   g. Cable News Network

_____ 8. HBO   h. Music Television

Compound Words

Choose a word from each box. Combine the words into a compound word and write the new word on the line.

Compound words are words made up of two or more words. Each is written as one word and has a special meaning that comes from the combination of words.

base	eye	news	weather
earth	house	up	week

ball	days	papers	witness
dates	man	quake	work

1. In the summer, you can watch a _____ game on TV every night.

2. My favorite _____ gives the forecast every morning on Channel 4.

3. We saw pictures on the news of the damage caused by the _____.

4. The news is on at 6 and 11, but there are _____ every hour, too.

5. Most soap operas are broadcast on _____, but not on Saturday and Sunday.

6. The news reporter interviewed an _____ to the accident.

7. Some people take a break from _____ to watch a soap opera.

8. Many people get more news from TV than from _____.

Prefix

The prefix *tele–* means *far.*

Choose a word from the box, add *tele–* to it, and write it on the line.

communications	phone	scope
graph	photo	vision

1. We looked at the stars through the _____.

2. He studied _____, and now he works with TV and radio.

3. My dinner is often interrupted by _____ calls.

4. He put a _____ lens on the camera before he took a picture of the boat in the distance.

5. Some people watch too much _____.

6. In the past, people used to send messages by _____.

Suffix

The suffix *–ise* indicates that a word is a verb.

Choose a verb from the box and write it on the line.

advertise	despise	improvise	surprise
compromise	exercise	supervise	televise

1. The station is going to _____ all of the baseball games.

2. Companies love to _____ their products during sitcoms.

3. At the fitness club, many people watch TV while they _____.

4. The actors on live TV sometimes have to _____.

5. I think the ending of that show will _____ you.

6. If we can't agree on what to watch, we will have to _____.

7. Parents should _____ children when they are watching TV.

8. Some people _____ that show, while others love it.

Antonyms

Choose an antonym from the box for each underlined word and write it on the line.

> boring   dramas   live   love
> daytime   funny   local   serious

1. I love to watch <u>comedies</u> on TV. I think _____ are boring.

2. Pete likes <u>serious</u> programs, but I only watch _____ ones.

3. Most news broadcasts are _____, but news magazines are usually <u>taped</u>.

4. Ed thinks sitcoms are <u>interesting</u>, but Pete thinks they are _____.

5. Most soap operas are on in the _____, but a few are on at <u>night</u>.

6. People feel strongly about soap operas. Those who don't _____ them usually <u>despise</u> them.

7. The <u>national</u> news comes on right after the _____ news.

8. Some shows on cable take a <u>humorous</u> look at _____ issues.

Collocations

> **We use many collocations with *turn* and a preposition to talk about TV and daily activities.**

Choose a preposition from the box and write it on the line. One of the words can be used more than once.

> down   into   off   on   up

1. If you can't hear the TV, you can turn _____ the volume.

2. If you watch TV for too long, you will turn _____ a couch potato.

3. That's too loud! Please turn it _____.

4. The program begins in a minute. I'll turn the TV _____ now.

5. Please turn the TV _____ when you leave the room.

6. I lost my TV remote again, but I'm sure it will turn _____ somewhere.

22   Lesson 2

Confusing Words

Circle the word that best completes
the sentence.

> **See** and **watch** both have to do with using your eyes.
> **See** means to use your eyes to receive images in a
> natural way, without thinking about it. **Watch** means to
> follow a moving image with your eyes, giving it your
> attention.

1. When I was a child, I didn't (see/watch) much TV.

2. When I came into the room, at first I didn't (see/watch) your new TV set. But then I
   noticed it after a few minutes.

3. I love to play soccer, but I don't like to sit in the stands and (see/watch) a game.

4. Where did you put the remote for the TV? I don't (see/watch) it anywhere.

5. That movie was so scary that I couldn't (see/watch) the end. I had to cover my eyes.

6. I like to (see/watch) the news while I'm eating dinner.

7. Do you have an antenna? I didn't (see/watch) one on your roof.

8. My mother (sees/watches) two game shows every evening.

Write *like(s)* or *would like* on the line.

> **Like** and **would like** look similar, but they have different
> meanings. **Like** means *enjoy*, while **would like** is the
> same as *want*. You can use an infinitive (*to* + verb) or a
> gerund (verb + *–ing*) after **like**. You can use an infinitive
> (*to* + verb) after **would like**.

9. Ed _____ watching TV more than Pete does.

10. Pete only _____ to watch the news.

11. I went into the shop and told the salesperson that I _____ to buy a new
    TV set.

12. I _____ to have cable TV, but I can't afford the monthly payment.

13. I _____ watching my favorite sitcoms with my friends.

14. Pete _____ to study telecommunications, but his grades aren't good
    enough.

15. Ed _____ going to the baseball stadium to watch baseball games.

16. Pete _____ talking to Ed about TV.

Context Clues

Choose a word from below each line
and write it on the line.

1. Companies buy commercials on TV in order to _____ their
   buy / advertise / improvise
   products.

2. Last night we turned on PBS and watched a _____ about the
   sitcom / soap opera / documentary
   origins of baseball. We learned a lot about the history of the sport.

3. I watched most of the local news last night. I saw the news and the sports, but I didn't see
   the _____.
   weather / drama / broadcast

4. Soap operas are a very popular form of _____ entertainment.
   weekend / weeknight / weekday

5. He doesn't have cable, so he has to put an _____ on the roof of
   advertisement / antenna / announcement
   his house.

6. The local news program on my favorite channel has the best
   _____, the best sports announcer, and the best movie reviews.
   reporters / cable / talk show

7. Actors often have to _____ on live TV when they don't have a
   advertise / improvise / televise
   script or when something goes wrong. They just make things up.

8. People like Ed think TV can be both _____ and entertaining.
   boring / commercial / informative
   They feel like they learn something from TV while they are enjoying themselves.

Parts of Speech

Identify the underlined words. Write *N* on the line if the word is a noun, and write *V* if it is a verb.

> **Many common vocabulary words can work either as nouns or verbs. Look for a noun after an adjective. Look for a verb after a modal like *can* or *will*.**

_____ 1. I watched an interesting <u>broadcast</u> last night.

_____ 2. I can't <u>set</u> the clock on my new video recorder.

_____ 3. The station will <u>show</u> that movie tomorrow.

_____ 4. I can <u>program</u> your VCR for you.

_____ 5. That was a funny <u>show</u>.

_____ 6. That network will <u>broadcast</u> the football championship game.

_____ 7. My TV is so small. I want to get a bigger <u>set</u>.

_____ 8. There was a fascinating <u>program</u> on TV last night.

Dictionary

Identify the part of speech of each underlined word. Write *N* or *V* on the line. Then look up the word in your dictionary. Choose and write the best definition.

_____ 1. Let's buy a new TV <u>set</u>.

definition: _____

_____ 2. I don't like this program. Can we change the <u>channel</u>?

definition: _____

_____ 3. The network is going to <u>air</u> that documentary without commercials.

definition: _____

_____ 4. After the storm, there was a <u>cable</u> on the ground in front of my apartment.

definition: _____

_____ 5. We watched your show last night. Tonight it is my <u>turn</u> to choose the show.

definition: _____

Crossword Puzzle

Fill in the puzzle with words from the box.

CNN	documentary	MTV	taped
comedies	eyewitnesses	NBC	telescope
commercials	housework	sitcoms	updates
compromise	live	surprise	watched

ACROSS

1. We _____ a baseball game on TV.
3. My favorite _____ come on every Thursday evening.
4. Most news broadcasts are _____.
7. The talk show is usually _____ a few days in advance.
9. I prefer _____ over dramas.
11. You need a _____ to see distant objects.
13. I think the end of the movie will _____ you.
14. _____ stands for the *National Broadcasting Company.*
15. My show was interrupted by several _____.
16. I like to take a break from my _____ and watch a daytime talk show.

DOWN

2. If we can't agree on what to watch, we will have to _____.
5. They like to interview _____ on the news.
6. Between news broadcasts there are hourly _____.
8. I watched a _____ on PBS about World War I.
10. _____ stands for *Music Television.*
12. _____ stands for *Cable News Network.*

Vocabulary in Context
Choose a word from the box and write it on the line.

antenna	broadcast	cable	entertains	informs

I love TV. I think it both _____ and _____ us. I live near a big
                              1   2

city, so several local channels _____ over the air. For many years I had an
                                        3

_____ on my roof. The signal was pretty clear. But then I decided that I
      4

wanted many more channels. I called the _____ company and they came
                                                    5

out and hooked me up to their system. Now I can be informed and entertained by nearly

100 channels!

down	into	off	on	up

My remote control is turning me _____ a couch potato. Here's what I do. I sit
                                        6

down on the couch with a snack. I use the remote to turn the TV _____. If I
                                                                        7

can't hear it, I hit a button to turn the volume _____. If someone yells that the
                                                        8

TV is too loud, no problem. I just use the remote to turn it _____. I usually fall
                                                                    9

asleep right there on the couch. After a while I wake up and turn the TV _____.
                                                                                10

advertise	compromise	despise	supervise	televise

I just _____ it when companies _____ junk food during
            11   12

children's shows. I think that TV networks should agree to _____ children's
                                                                    13

shows with no commercials. Or maybe they can _____ and only show
                                                        14

commercials for healthy food. If the networks don't do something about the commercials,

I think parents should _____ their children when they are watching TV.
                                15

A Letter

In this lesson, you will work with words about writing and sending letters. Read this story about a letter that Helen had to write.

Last month Helen had a complaint about a local department store. She bought a watch there. The watch broke the first time that she wore it. The clerk at the jewelry counter refused to refund Helen's money, and Helen thought the clerk was very rude. Helen's friend Rosa told her to write a letter to the department store. Helen thought that was a good idea, but she had never written a formal business letter. Rosa offered to tell her how to do it.

First, Helen had to write her address, the date, and the address of the department store at the top of the paper. Then she wrote the **greeting**. She didn't have the name of a specific person at the department store, so she wrote "To whom it may concern." Then she wrote the **body** of the letter. She **composed** two paragraphs explaining the problem. Then she needed a **closing**. Rosa told her to use the word *sincerely* for her closing and then to **sign** her name.

When the letter was written, Helen **folded** it and put it in an **envelope**. She **addressed** the envelope carefully. She double checked the ZIP Code. Then Helen made sure to put the correct **postage** on the envelope. She also put her **return address** in the upper left corner, just in case the post office couldn't **deliver** the letter.

Helen is glad she sent the letter. She hopes that the department store will **respond** to her complaint soon.

Definitions

Write each word or phrase next to its definition.

address	compose	fold	respond
body	deliver	greeting	return address
closing	envelope	postage	sign

_____ 1. to say or write something as a reply or answer

_____ 2. to bring to a particular person or place

_____ 3. to write your name in a distinctive way on a letter or document to prove that you wrote it or agree with it

_____ 4. words written at the beginning of a letter that show respect or pleasure

_____ 5. a folded paper covering for a letter or other papers

_____ 6. to write something, thinking carefully as you write

_____ 7. to bend something so that one part lies on top of another part

_____ 8. the end or last part of something

_____ 9. the largest, central, or main part of something

_____ 10. the amount of money charged to send a letter or package by mail

_____ 11. to write information on an envelope, including name, street, city, and state, that tells where to send it

_____ 12. the name, street, city, and state of the person who sends a letter, usually written on the front of an envelope in the upper left corner

State Name Abbreviations

Match each abbreviation with the state that it represents.

When you address a letter, always use a two-letter state abbreviation. If you don't know an abbreviation, you can ask at the post office. When you read a state abbreviation, you say the whole name. For example, when you read *NY* you say *New York.*

_____ 1. CA   a. Florida

_____ 2. FL   b. Virginia

_____ 3. PA   c. Colorado

_____ 4. TX   d. Illinois

_____ 5. AZ   e. California

_____ 6. VA   f. Pennsylvania

_____ 7. IL   g. Arizona

_____ 8. CO   h. Texas

Compound Words

Choose a word from each box. Combine the words into a compound word and write the new word on the line.

Compound words are words made up of two or more words. Each is written as one word and has a special meaning that comes from the combination of words.

birth	grand	note	some
dead	hand	post	waste

basket	card	father	thing
book	day	line	writing

1. If you have _____ important to tell me, write me a letter.

2. For my best friend's _____, I sent a card and a long letter.

3. My _____ is hard to read, so I like to type the address on the envelope.

4. If you want the letter to arrive before the _____, you have to mail it today.

5. I write a letter to my _____ every week.

6. She composed the letter in her _____, and then she copied it onto nice stationery.

7. When I opened the letter, I threw the envelope in the _____.

8. When you go on vacation, please send me a _____.

Prefix

Choose a word from the box, add *post–* to it, and write it on the line.

date	operative	season	test
game	script	secondary	war

1. We add a _____ at the end of a letter by writing *P.S.* and an additional message.

2. A high school is a secondary school, and a college is a _____ school.

3. He took a pretest, then he studied, and then he took a _____.

4. After they played, they had a _____ celebration.

5. After the operation, the patient had a lot of _____ pain.

6. After the team finished all of its regular games, it played a _____ game.

7. During the war the country had a lot of problems, but the _____ economy was good.

8. If you _____ a check, you write a date that is after today's date.

Suffix

Choose an adjective from the box and write it on the line.

central	emotional	national	personal
comical	formal	optional	professional

1. If you are writing a _____ letter, you should type it, but you can hand write an informal one.

2. Don't write *sincerely* as a closing in a _____ letter.

3. I laughed at the _____ parts of the letter.

4. The body is the _____ part of the letter.

5. Your letter will look more _____ if you use the company's paper.

6. The ZIP Code system is a _____ system.

7. When writing a complaint letter to a company, try not to be _____.

8. The greeting is not _____; you must have one.

Exercise 6

Synonyms

Choose a word from the box with about the same meaning as each
underlined word or phrase. Then write it on the line.

> compose   personal   salutation   stamp
> formal   response   sincerely

1. Some people can _____ on a word processor, but I like to <u>write</u> by hand.

2. The _____, or <u>greeting</u>, usually begins with the word *dear.*

3. When you close your letter, you can write _____ or *yours truly.*

4. It's acceptable to handwrite an <u>informal</u>, _____ letter.

5. If you are writing a _____ letter, such as a <u>business</u> letter, then you should type it.

6. If you send a letter to a company, you can expect a _____ within six weeks. Sometimes, however, companies don't <u>answer</u> letters.

7. I need to put a _____ on this letter, but I don't know how much the <u>postage</u> will be.

Exercise 7

Collocations

Choose a word from the box to
complete each collocation below.

> **English speakers use many collocations of two or three words when talking about mailing a letter.**

> address   box   first-class   return
> apartment   Code   post

1. If you need to weigh a letter, you should go to the _____ office.

2. Don't mail a letter without the ZIP _____.

3. You should pay a little extra to send the package by _____ mail.

4. Please include the _____ number in your address.

5. Don't forget to put your _____ address on the envelope.

6. If you move, you will have to fill out a change-of- _____ card at the post office.

7. Some people have a P.O. _____ number instead of a street address.

Confusing Words

Write *write* or *right* on the line.

> *Write* and *right* sound the same, so they are often confused in writing. *Write* is a verb that usually means *to form letters or numbers with a pen or pencil. Right* can be an adjective, an adverb, a noun, or a verb. It is most commonly an adjective meaning *correct* or *true,* or an adjective meaning *the opposite of left.*

1. When I hold a pen, I use my _____ hand.

2. Be sure you have the _____ street number for the address.

3. I need to _____ a letter to my grandmother.

4. My cousin can _____ with either hand.

5. Don't forget to _____ your return address on the envelope.

6. Put your return address on the left side and the stamp on the _____.

7. Please make certain that you have the _____ ZIP Code.

8. Please _____ the ZIP Code clearly after the state.

Circle the word that best completes the sentence.

> *Bend* and *fold* have similar meanings but are used to express different ideas. You can *bend* a part of your body or an object. When you *bend* something, you push or press it into a curved shape. When you *fold* something, you bend it so that one part completely covers another part. You can fold objects like paper or clothing. You can *fold* something in half, but you can't *bend* it in half.

9. My knee hurts and I can't (bend/fold) it.

10. You should (bend/fold) your shirts before you put them in the drawer.

11. He (bent/folded) the letter several times before he put it in the envelope.

12. If you try to (bend/fold) your pencil, it will break.

13. When I fell off my bike, I (bent/folded) the front wheel.

14. She ruined the photograph because she (bent/folded) it in half to fit it in the envelope.

15. When I hurt my finger, I couldn't (bend/fold) it.

16. I didn't have a bookmark, so I (bent/folded) the corner of the page to mark my place.

Context Clues

Choose a word from below each line
and write it on the line.

It is often possible to guess a missing word from the
context of a sentence. When you rely on context, you use
what you know about the other words in a sentence to
help you guess the word.

1. He had the street address, the city, and the state. He had to go to the post office to look

   up the _____ before he could mail the letter.
   return address / ZIP Code / postage stamp

2. It is appropriate to use the word _____ in the greeting of a
   sincerely / love / dear

   business letter.

3. In the closing of a business letter, it is customary to put your _____
   signature / return address / greeting

   above your typed name.

4. If you need to write a/an _____ letter, be sure to type it.
   personal / business / informal

5. The letter carrier has to sort and _____ the mail.
   deliver / respond / compose

6. After you write and sign a letter, fold it and put it in the _____.
   postage stamp / ZIP Code / envelope

7. I received a/an _____ from my cousin today. It had a picture of a
   letter / postcard / envelope
   beautiful beach on the front. On the back, she told me about her great vacation in Mexico.

8. If you write a letter of complaint to a company, be sure to include your address and phone

   number so that the company can _____ to you.
   respond / compose / receive

Parts of Speech

Identify the underlined words. Write
Adj. on the line if the word is an
adjective, and write *Adv.* if it is an
adverb.

Adjectives modify nouns, and adverbs usually modify action verbs. You can usually make an adverb from an adjective by adding *–ly,* but some words use the same word for both forms. Four of these words that work as both adjectives and adverbs are *fast, early, hard,* and *straight.* Look for an adjective before a noun or after *be.* Look for an adverb after an action verb.

_____ 1. That letter carrier is a <u>fast</u> walker.

_____ 2. Our letter carrier never comes <u>early</u>.

_____ 3. Letter carriers work <u>hard</u>.

_____ 4. I hope the letter comes in the <u>early</u> delivery.

_____ 5. If you choose express mail, your letter will go <u>straight</u> to its destination.

_____ 6. It is <u>hard</u> to memorize a lot of ZIP Codes.

_____ 7. Be sure to write the address in <u>straight</u> lines.

_____ 8. The mail truck doesn't go <u>fast</u>.

Dictionary

Identify the part of speech of each underlined word. Write *N* or *V* on
the line. Then look up the word in your dictionary. Choose and write
the best definition.

_____ 1. Be sure to <u>date</u> your letter so people will know when you wrote it.

definition: _____

_____ 2. The supervisor <u>addressed</u> the group of mail carriers in their monthly meeting.

definition: _____

_____ 3. To cut a straight line, bend the paper then cut it along the <u>fold</u>.

definition: _____

_____ 4. The department assistant <u>stamps</u> the letters with the word *received* and the date when he opens them.

definition: _____

_____ 5. Be sure to <u>sign</u> your letter before you mail it.

definition: _____

Crossword Puzzle

Fill in the puzzle with words from the box.

AZ	compose	folded	postscript	Sincerely	VA
body	deadline	personal	professional	stationery	wastebasket
carrier	envelope	postage	respond	TX	ZIP

ACROSS

6. *P.S.* stands for _____.
7. She wrote three paragraphs in the _____ of her letter.
9. Put your return address on the _____.
11. The postal abbreviation for *Arizona* is _____.
12. She _____ the letter several times before she put it in the envelope.
15. _____ is a good word to use in a closing.
16. The postal abbreviation for *Texas* is _____.
17. The letter _____ on my street walks fast.

DOWN

1. If you write a letter, it may take a week or two for the person to _____.
2. Throw the envelope away in the _____.
3. A _____ Code is written after the state abbreviation.
4. A company uses _____ for its letters.
5. The clerk will weigh your letter and tell you how much _____ you need.
6. It looks more _____ if you type a letter.
8. You need to have some letters postmarked before the _____.
10. The postal abbreviation for *Virginia* is _____.
13. He didn't want to use a computer for the _____ letter.
14. It's hard to _____ a letter on a computer.

Vocabulary in Context

Choose a word from the box and write it on the line.

| body | compose | envelope | folded | greeting | signed | sincerely |

Helen wrote a letter to apply for a new job. She used the manager's name in the

_____. Then, in the _____ of the letter, she wrote about her
1   2

experience. It took a long time to _____ three paragraphs. Helen wrote
3

"_____" and _____ her name. Then she
4   5

_____ the letter and put it in the _____.
6   7

| box | carriers | change | Code | office | postage |

It was a busy day at my local post _____. First, all of the letter
8

_____ came in to sort the mail for their routes. Then the customers started to
9

come in. One person wanted to rent a P.O. _____. Someone else needed to
10

look up a ZIP _____. Three people needed to fill out _____ -
11   12

of-address cards. A lot of people needed to find out how much _____ to put
13

on letters and packages.

| AZ | CO | PA | TX | VA |

Tom writes a lot of letters, so he has memorized the postal abbreviations for a lot of states.

For example, it's easy to remember that _____ stands for *Texas.* It's harder to remember that
14

_____ stands for *Pennsylvania*, and that _____ stands for *Arizona.* He gets confused about
15   16

Virginia and can't remember that it is _____. Tom's brother just moved to Colorado, and Tom
17

is happy because he already knows that the postal abbreviation for Colorado is _____.
18

Air Travel

In this lesson, you will work with words about airplanes and airports. Read this conversation between Susan and Bob.

Bob: Hi, Susan. What's up? You look worried.

Susan: Hi, Bob. Could you tell that I'm worried? I'm flying back home tomorrow to visit my grandmother. I'm nervous because I haven't been on an airplane since I was a little girl.

Bob: Well, flying can be a **hassle** these days, but there's really nothing to worry about.

Susan: That makes me feel better. But why is it a hassle?

Bob: Well, you are going to stand in a lot of lines. Your first line will be as soon as you **reach** the **terminal**.

Susan: What do I do then?

Bob: You show your identification to the ticket **agent** and get a boarding **pass**. That person will take any **luggage** that you want to **check**, too. After that, you stand in another line.

Susan: What's that line for?

Bob: That's when you go through the security **checkpoint**. The agents at that checkpoint will x-ray your carry-on bags and ask you to walk through a metal **detector**.

Susan: That doesn't sound so bad. Then what?

Bob: Then you **proceed** to the gate number that is written on your boarding pass. You wait there for the plane.

Susan: What happens next?

Bob: The gate agent will tell you when to **board** the plane. When you get to your seat, buckle your seatbelt and get ready to watch the safety demonstration that the flight attendants will present.

Susan: Thanks a lot, Bob. I feel better knowing what to expect.

Definitions

Write each word or phrase next to its definition.

agent	check	hassle	proceed
board	checkpoint	luggage	reach
buckle	detector	pass	terminal

_____ 1. a machine that finds or measures something

_____ 2. a printed card or paper that gives a person permission to enter

_____ 3. a large building where people go before they get on an airplane or a bus

_____ 4. to fasten or join together a device with two ends

_____ 5. to arrive at a place

_____ 6. to leave an object in a place, to either keep it safe or put it on a plane

_____ 7. a person who works in an official capacity and has the authority to do certain actions

_____ 8. a place where an official person examines people, objects, and documents

_____ 9. something that is annoying, unpleasant, or harder than it should be

_____ 10. to get into or on something that is used for transportation

_____ 11. to go forward or move ahead

_____ 12. suitcases and other bags that you use to carry things when you are traveling

Agency Initializations

Match each initialization with the agency that it stands for.

When you go to an airport or get on an airplane, you may notice several initializations that refer to U.S. government agencies. You can explain initializations with sentences using *stands for.*

_____ 1. TSA   a. Federal Aviation Administration

_____ 2. FAA   b. Customs and Border Protection

_____ 3. DOT   c. Department of Homeland Security

_____ 4. DEA   d. Transportation Security Administration

_____ 5. DHS   e. Drug Enforcement Administration

_____ 6. CBP   f. Department of Transportation

Compound Words

Choose a word from each box. Combine the words into a compound word and write the new word on the line.

Compound words are words made up of two or more words. Each is written as one word and has a special meaning that comes from the combination of words.

air	cab	pass	thunder
back	good	sky	walk

bye	driver	port	storm
craft	pack	scrapers	ways

1. If you need to show I.D., you may show your _____.

2. If there is a _____, the plane might not take off.

3. You can carry your _____ on the plane.

4. We saw the _____ in Chicago when we landed.

5. The _____ dropped me at the door of the terminal.

6. Many airports have moving _____ and escalators.

7. If friends come to the airport with you, you have to say _____ before the TSA checkpoint.

8. The flight attendant will show you the exits on the _____.

Prefix

Discuss the meanings of the words in the box. Then choose a word from the box and write it on the line.

unicycle	**union**	**unite**
uniforms	**unique**	**universal**

1. The flight attendants have to wear blue _____.

2. English is the _____ language of air traffic controllers.

3. The new company wants its service to be _____ so it will be different from all of the others.

4. Two companies are going to _____ and form one company.

5. The clown in the circus rode on a _____.

6. The workers formed a _____ so that they can communicate to the managers with one voice.

Exercise 5: **Word Builder**

Suffix

The suffix *–ant* often indicates that a word refers to a person.

Choose a word from the box and write it on the line.

accountant	**attendants**	**immigrant**	**occupants**
assistant	**contestant**	**inhabitants**	**servants**

1. There are two or three flight _____ on the airplane.

2. A sign in the restaurant tells how many _____ are allowed.

3. A copilot is like an _____ to the pilot.

4. The people who live in a city or town are called its _____.

5. The _____ on the TV game show won an airline ticket to Hawaii.

6. In the past, rich people often had many _____ to wait on them.

7. The company's _____ keeps records of money earned and spent.

8. The _____ had to fill out some papers for the DHS.

Synonyms

Choose a word from the box that means about the same as each underlined
word or phrase. Write the word on the line.

aircraft	baggage	fastened	restroom
arrived	departed	pilot	traveler

1. Most people check their <u>luggage</u> then pick it up at the _____ claim.

2. My cousin's flight _____ on time, but my sister's plane <u>landed</u> an hour late.

3. You should <u>buckle</u> your seat belt and keep it _____ during the flight.

4. All <u>passengers</u> must have I.D.. A TSA agent might ask a _____ for I.D. at any time.

5. Find out where the exits are on your _____. Not all <u>airplanes</u> are the same.

6. The _____ on a plane is often called a <u>lavatory</u>.

7. My first flight <u>took off</u> on time, but the second flight _____ late.

8. Mr. Sparks knows how to <u>fly</u> an airplane, but he can't _____ a helicopter.

Collocations

We use many collocations with prepositions to talk about flying on planes.

Choose a word from the box and write it
on the line. One of the words can be used more than once.

at	in	off	on	out	up

1. As soon as you get _____ the plane, you should buckle your seatbelt.

2. Don't stand _____ when the seatbelt sign is lit.

3. After the plane takes _____, the flight attendant will come by.

4. You usually don't need to check _____ at the gate.

5. On an international flight, you have to fill _____ some forms for Customs.

6. Be sure you have all of your carry-on items when you get _____ the plane.

7. Passengers have to turn _____ all electronic equipment before the plane takes off.

8. Don't unbuckle your seatbelt until the plane arrives _____ the gate.

Confusing Words

Fill in each sentence with a form of *fly, drive, ride,* or *sail.*

> *Fly, drive, ride,* and *sail* all have to do with controlling a vehicle. We *fly* something in the air. We *drive* a vehicle with four wheels and *ride* one with one, two, or three wheels. We *sail* on the water.

1. The clown ___rides___ a unicycle every night in the circus.

2. The military pilot ___flew___ an experimental jet.

3. Do you know how to ___ride___ a motorcycle?

4. On my vacation last summer, I ___sailed___ a boat in the lake.

5. My brother ___drives___ a taxicab.

6. I saw many people who were ___riding___ scooters in the city.

7. He ___sails___ a yacht in the Caribbean every summer.

8. I don't know how to ___fly___ an airplane.

9. Can you ___ride___ a bicycle to school?

10. I want to learn how to ___drive___ a bus.

11. The stunt pilot ___flew___ a biplane over the circus.

12. Elderly people can't ___drive___ cars if their vision is very poor.

13. They ___sailed___ the ship into the harbor during the storm.

14. They say you never forget how to ___drive/ride___ a bicycle.

15. Does he know how to ___fly___ the new aircraft?

16. The boy _____ his bike to school every day.

17. How many pilots can _____ that new jet?

18. Last year I _____ a van from Florida to Maine.

19. How old were you when you started to _____ a tricycle?

20. I want to learn how to _____ a plane.

Context Clues

Choose a word from below each line
and write it on the line.

1. At the airport, I stood in a long line with a lot of other _____. We
   passengers / flight attendants / pilots
   had our boarding passes and our I.D. cards in our hands.

2. When I arrived at the airport, I walked up to a counter and talked to a

   _____. I told her my name and where I was going, and I gave
   flight attendant / ticket agent / copilot
   her my credit card.

3. After I checked my _____ with the ticket agent, I had to stand in a
   luggage / passenger / seatbelt
   long security line.

4. I had to show my I.D. and my boarding pass at the TSA _____.
   gate / terminal / checkpoint

5. If the pilot turns off the seatbelt sign, that means you can stand up, walk around, and use

   the _____ on the plane.
   gate / luggage / lavatory

6. My brother is taking lessons at his local airport because he wants to learn how to

   _____ an airplane.
   fly / drive / ride

7. You can't carry your big suitcase on the plane. You have to _____
   fasten / board / check
   it with the ticket agent when you arrive at the airport.

8. Please stay seated with your seatbelt fastened. Don't stand up until the airplane

   _____ the gate and the pilot turns off the seatbelt sign.
   reaches / checks / buckles

Parts of Speech

Identify the underlined words. Write *V* on the line if the word is a verb, and write *Adj.* if it is an adjective.

> Many common vocabulary words that end in *–ed* can work either as verbs or as adjectives. Look for a verb after a subject and before an object. Look for an adjective before a noun.

_____ 1. I <u>checked</u> my bags when I arrived at the airport.

_____ 2. You can only pass through the TSA checkpoint with a <u>printed</u> boarding pass.

_____ 3. The TSA agent <u>checked</u> my boarding pass.

_____ 4. The ticked agent <u>printed</u> my boarding pass.

_____ 5. If you need to carry scissors, put them in your <u>checked</u> luggage.

_____ 6. The gate agent <u>approved</u> my upgrade to first class.

_____ 7. Is a driver's license an <u>approved</u> form of identification?

_____ 8. Pets like cats and dogs usually ride with the <u>checked</u> baggage.

Dictionary

Identify the part of speech of each underlined word. Write *N* or *V* on the line. Then look up the word in your dictionary. Choose and write the best definition.

_____ 1. The flight attendant has to be tall enough to <u>reach</u> the overhead bins.

definition: _____

_____ 2. If you can't remember the gate number, you should <u>check</u> your boarding pass.

definition: _____

_____ 3. There are large <u>boards</u> in the airport that give departure and arrival information.

definition: _____

_____ 4. After you <u>pass</u> the security checkpoint, you may still need to show your I.D..

definition: _____

_____ 5. If you park by the door of the airport terminal, you will get a <u>ticket</u>.

definition: _____

Crossword Puzzle

Fill in the puzzle with words from the box.

assistant	checkpoint	landed	passport	uniforms
attendants	detector	lavatory	terminal	up
board	DHS	luggage	thunderstorm	walkway
buckle	FAA	off	TSA	

ACROSS

2. It's a long walk through the _____ to the gate.
3. Don't stand _____ if the seatbelt sign is on.
5. Do you have any _____ to check?
8. My plane _____ at 4:00 but I didn't get home until 6.
9. _____ stands for *Transportation Security Administration.*
12. A copilot is like an _____ to the pilot.
13. You will need your _____ if you fly to another country.
14. The flight attendant will tell you to turn _____ your electronic equipment.
16. Most airline employees have to wear _____.
17. _____ stands for *Federal Aviation Administration.*
18. You need to walk through the metal _____.

DOWN

1. Please _____ your seatbelt.
2. It can be dangerous to fly through a _____.
4. Each flight has several flight _____.
6. Show your boarding pass and I.D. at the _____.
7. You can't use the _____ if the seatbelt sign is on.
10. _____ stands for *Department of Homeland Security.*
11. If you get tired, you can get on the moving _____.
15. You can wait at the gate until you _____ the airplane.

Vocabulary in Context

Choose a word from the box and write it on the line.

| backpack | boarded | checkpoint | fastened | gate | hassle | terminal |

Susan flew back home last week. She had a great experience in the airport. It wasn't a

_____ after all. As soon as she arrived at the _____, she
　　　　1　　　　　　　　　　　　　　　　　　　　　　　　　　　　　　2

checked her bags and walked through the TSA _____. She waited at the
　　　　　　　　　　　　　　　　　　　　　　　　　　　　3

_____ for about 15 minutes. After she _____ the plane and
　　　4　　　　　　　　　　　　　　　　　　　　　　　　　　　　　　5

put her _____ under the seat in front of her, she _____ her
　　　　　　6　　　　　　　　　　　　　　　　　　　　　　　　　　　　　7

seatbelt and relaxed.

| drove | flew | rode | sailed | took |

I used every kind of transportation available to me on my vacation last summer. First, I

_____ a taxi to the airport. I _____ to Tampa for my vacation.
　　　8　　　　　　　　　　　　　　　　　　　　　9

I rented a car for a week and _____ all around the west coast of Florida. One
　　　　　　　　　　　　　　　　　　10

day, I borrowed a bicycle at the hotel and _____ along a bike path. Another
　　　　　　　　　　　　　　　　　　　　　　　　11

day I visited a friend who has a boat and we _____ on Tampa Bay. It was a
　　　　　　　　　　　　　　　　　　　　　　　　12

great vacation.

| departed | landed | pilot | taken off |

I flew to Chicago last month and had a great flight. The plane _____ on
　　　　　　　　　　　　　　　　　　　　　　　　　　　13

schedule. In fact, after we were in the air the _____ announced that we had
　　　　　　　　　　　　　　　　　　　14

_____ three minutes early. We arrived on schedule. When we
　　15

_____, the flight attendant said, "Welcome to Chicago."
　　16

A Restaurant

In this lesson, you will work with words about restaurants. Read this story about Alice's birthday celebration.

Alice's birthday was last week. Her friends took her to a new restaurant called Surf and Turf. They made a **reservation** for 7:30. A group of 10 friends attended the celebration.

When Alice's group arrived, the **hostess** greeted them. She **seated** them in the dining room and gave each person a **menu**. Soon, a **waitress** came over to them. She took their **beverage** order. She asked them about **appetizers**. Everyone ordered a drink, and the group ordered several appetizers to share.

Surf and Turf is not a fancy restaurant. The waiters and waitresses wear black pants, white shirts, and red **aprons**. The tables have simple white tablecloths. There is a red rose in a vase on each table. Alice thought that it was the perfect place for a quiet celebration.

While everyone was enjoying the appetizers, each person selected an **entrée**. Since Surf and Turf is famous for seafood and beef, everyone ordered either fish or steak. Each entrée came with two side dishes. They chose potatoes or rice, and a vegetable or salad.

A **server** helped the waitress bring out the food when it was ready. Everything was delicious. Alice and her friends asked the waitress to give their compliments to the **chef**.

Soon everyone was finished. It was time for birthday cake. All of the waiters and waitresses, the servers, the **busboys**, and the hostess sang to Alice when they brought out the cake. Alice had a wonderful time at Surf and Turf on her birthday.

Definitions

Write each word or phrase next to its definition.

appetizer	busboy	hostess / host	seat
apron	chef	menu	server
beverage	entrée	reservation	waitress / waiter

_____ 1. the head cook in a restaurant

_____ 2. a piece of clothing that covers the front part of your body, is tied around your waist, and keeps your clothes clean, especially when you are working with food

_____ 3. a request to save a table for you at a restaurant

_____ 4. to arrange for someone to sit somewhere or to lead a person to a place to sit

_____ 5. a person who takes orders and serves food and drinks in a restaurant

_____ 6. the main dish of a meal at dinner or lunch

_____ 7. a small dish eaten before the main part of a meal

_____ 8. a person who greets customers in a restaurant and takes them to their table

_____ 9. a person who takes dirty dishes from the tables back to the kitchen in a restaurant

_____ 10. a list of foods served at a restaurant

_____ 11. a person who carries food to a table in a restaurant

_____ 12. a formal word for a hot or cold drink, usually not water

Exercise 2

Measurement Abbreviations

Match the abbreviation with the word or words that it represents.

When a chef measures ingredients, he or she often uses abbreviations for measurements. When you read an abbreviation, you say the whole word. For example, when you read *oz.* you say *ounce.*

_____ 1. lb.   a. tablespoon

_____ 2. qt.   b. pound

_____ 3. gal.   c. gallon

_____ 4. oz.   d. fluid ounce

_____ 5. pt.   e. ounce

_____ 6. tsp.   f. pint

_____ 7. fl. oz.   g. teaspoon

_____ 8. tbsp.   h. quart

Exercise 3

Compound Words

Choose a word from each box. Combine the words into a compound word and write the new word on the line.

Compound words are words made up of two or more words. Each is written as one word and has a special meaning that comes from the combination of words.

black	cheese	in	table
bus	dish	rest	tea

board	burger	cups	room
boy	cloths	doors	washers

1. The customer asked the hostess to show him where the _____ was.

2. When we were finished eating, the _____ took away the dirty dishes.

3. They have three large _____ that clean the plates and glasses automatically.

4. That restaurant has pink linen _____ and napkins on each table.

5. We drank from delicate china _____.

6. In that informal restaurant, the chef writes the menu on a _____ every day.

7. I ordered a _____ and fries for lunch.

8. They have tables in the garden, but we ate _____ because it looked like rain.

Prefix

> The prefix *under–* can mean *less than appropriate or desirable.*

Choose a word from the box, add *under-* to it, and write it on the line.

cooked	estimated	rated	used
charged	paid	sized	weight

1. When we got the bill, we noticed that the waitress had _____ us.

2. There is an _____ room in the restaurant that they are going to turn into a bar.

3. I sent the hamburger back to the kitchen because it was _____.

4. That child looks so thin. I think she is _____.

5. The chef _____ the number of customers and didn't order enough food.

6. That restaurant is _____. It is better than the critics claimed.

7. Many waitresses say that they are _____ and overworked.

8. The kitchen is _____, so they need to make it bigger.

Suffix

> The suffix *–ess* often indicates that a word is a noun that refers to a woman.

Choose a noun from the box and write it on the line.

actress	heiress	princess	waitress
goddesses	hostess	stewardesses	

1. Who won the award for best _____ this year?

2. We gave our order to the _____.

3. The _____ inherited millions of dollars.

4. In the movie, the king married a _____.

5. We used to call flight attendants _____.

6. I read some stories about Greek gods and _____.

7. The _____ showed us to our table.

Synonyms

Choose a word from the box that has about the same meaning as each
underlined word or phrase. Write the word on the line.

> alcohol   chef   entrées   restrooms
> beverage   entrance   ordered   served

1. The hostess stood by the _____ to greet people as they came in the <u>door</u>.

2. She went to school to learn to be a <u>cook</u>, and now she is a _____ in a hotel.

3. First the waiter <u>brought</u> our drinks, and later he _____ the food.

4. I <u>asked for</u> a hamburger, but the waitress thought I had _____ a
   cheeseburger.

5. They don't have a <u>liquor</u> license, so they can't serve _____.

6. When she took our _____ order, we told her what we wanted to <u>drink</u>.

7. Look at the list of _____ to decide which <u>main dish</u> to order.

8. We asked for the <u>ladies' room</u>, and he told us that the _____ were
   downstairs.

Collocations

> We use many collocations of two or three words when
> we talk about restaurants.

Choose a word from the box to complete
each collocation below.

> area   dining   on   shakers
> counter   dishes   order

1. Everything in Scarlet's Place is red. Even the salt _____ are red.

2. In that fancy restaurant, four people waited _____ us at the same time.

3. We sat in the waiting _____ until our table was ready.

4. There is a small _____ room, with only a dozen tables.

5. You get two side _____ with your entrée.

6. If you want to eat at home, pick up your food at the take-out _____.

7. The hostess told us that a waiter would take our _____ soon.

Confusing Words

Write *on* or *for* on the line.

> *Wait* is a verb that has more than one meaning when you talk about a restaurant, depending on the preposition that follows it. *Wait on* means *to serve a customer,* and *wait for* means *to stay in a place or situation until some expected event happens.*

1. We waited 45 minutes _____ our table.

2. The bartender waited _____ us at the bar.

3. Which person waited _____ you?

4. If you want the chef's special, you'll wait an hour _____ it.

5. We waited _____ a table outside since the weather was so nice.

6. Two waitresses and the host waited _____ the large party.

7. When we were ready to leave, we waited 20 minutes _____ our check.

8. If you are pleased with the way she waited _____ you, leave a big tip.

Circle the word that best completes the sentence.

> *Wait* and *weight* sound the same, so it is easy to confuse them in writing. *Wait* can be a verb or a noun. As a verb, it means *to stay in a place or situation until some expected event happens.* As a noun it refers to *the period of time that you stay in the place or situation.* *Weight* is a noun that describes how heavy something is.

9. How long is the (wait/weight) for a table there?

10. I don't like to (wait/weight) for my food.

11. The steaks are sold by (wait/weight), so the bigger steaks are more expensive.

12. You can (wait/weight) in the bar if you want.

13. The chef put the fish on the scale to find out the (wait/weight).

14. If you eat in restaurants very often you might gain (wait/weight).

15. She told us that the (wait/weight) would be 45 minutes.

16. If you don't want to (wait/weight) for a table, you can get take out.

Context Clues

Choose a word from below each line
and write it on the line.

It is often possible to guess a missing word from the
context of the sentence. When you rely on context, you
use what you know about the other words in the
sentence to help you guess the word.

1. The waiter told us that we could order one of the chef's specials, or we could order

   something from the _____.
   menu / tablecloth / beverage

2. We thought that the food was delicious, so we asked our waitress to tell the

   _____ how pleased we were.
   hostess / busboy / chef

3. Before we left the restaurant, I wanted to wash my hands and brush my hair. I asked the

   hostess to direct me to the _____.
   waiting area / bar / restroom

4. The busboy stacked the dirty dishes next to the _____ in the
   dishwasher / dining room / restroom

   kitchen.

5. The hostess _____ us at a nice table near a window and
   waited / served / seated
   handed us each a menu.

6. When the waiter brought our drinks, he told us that he would be back in a minute to take

   our _____.
   side dish / order / reservation

7. Our waiter asked us if we would like to start with a/an _____,
   appetizer / reservation / check
   or if we were ready to order our entrées.

8. We noticed a mistake on our check. We told the waitress that we thought she had

   _____ us.
   underpaid / undercharged / underrated

Parts of Speech

Identify the underlined words. Write *N*
on the line if the word is a noun, and
write *V* if it is a verb.

Many words that we use when talking about restaurants
can work either as nouns or verbs. Look for a noun after
the or *a*. Look for a verb after *to.*

_____   1.   I prefer a <u>seat</u> near the window.

_____   2.   He learned how to <u>cook</u> in France.

_____   3.   Did you order a <u>drink</u> before I arrived?

_____   4.   I thought the hostess was going to <u>seat</u> us by the kitchen.

_____   5.   I saw the <u>cook</u> through the door of the kitchen.

_____   6.   The <u>wait</u> for a table at that popular restaurant is over an hour.

_____   7.   Is she going to <u>drink</u> soda or iced tea?

_____   8.   I am too hungry to <u>wait</u> for my entrée. Let's get an appetizer.

Dictionary

Identify the part of speech of each underlined word. Write *N* or *V* on
the line. Then look up the word in your dictionary. Choose and write
the best definition.

_____   1.   The young man's job is to <u>bus</u> the tables and fill water glasses.

   definition: _____

_____   2.   We had to stand in the waiting area because there were no <u>seats</u>.

   definition: _____

_____   3.   The first time we tried that restaurant, the food was terrible and the service was
        slow. That's why we had <u>reservations</u> and doubts about going back a second time.

   definition: _____

_____   4.   Everything in Scarlet's Place is red. Even the <u>dishes</u> and glasses are red.

   definition: _____

_____   5.   I <u>ordered</u> iced tea, but the waiter brought me lemonade.

   definition: _____

Crossword Puzzle

Fill in the puzzle with words from the box.

actresses	blackboard	entrance	Lb.	reservation	underestimated
appetizers	busboy	Gal.	liquor	Tsp.	underrated
beverage	dishwasher	hostess	out	waitress	

ACROSS

2. The chef writes the specials on a _____ near the entrance.
4. We ordered take-_____ food so we could eat at home.
9. The restaurant has pictures of actors and _____ who have eaten there.
10. The _____ took the dirty dishes to the kitchen.
11. For your _____, you can choose soda or iced tea.
12. The _____ took our order.
13. The _____ greeted us at the door.
14. _____ is the abbreviation for *teaspoon.*
15. The waiter served the _____ and salads first.
17. The hostess met us at the _____.

DOWN

1. That restaurant is _____. It is better than the guidebook said it was.
3. The restaurant needs a _____ license in order to serve alcohol.
5. We _____ the cost of the dinner so we didn't have enough money to pay the check.
6. The _____ uses water that is hot enough to kill germs.
7. We made a _____ for 7:00.
8. _____ is the abbreviation for *pound.*
16. _____ is the abbreviation for *gallon.*

Vocabulary in Context

Choose a word from the box and write it on the line. Use a capital
letter if necessary.

busboys	chef	cooks	hostesses	Servers	waitresses

The restaurant employs dozens of people. There are _____ who greet
1

customers, and waiters and _____ who take orders. There is a
2

_____ who is in charge in the kitchen. He or she is assisted by several
3

_____. _____ and _____ work in the dining
4   5   6

room. They help with serving the food and clearing the tables.

lb.	oz.	pt.	qt.	tsp.	tbsp.

The chef has all of his recipes written in a notebook. When he hired a new assistant, he had to

explain a lot of abbreviations used in the recipes. He told the assistant that _____ stands for
7

teaspoon and that _____ stands for tablespoon. It's important not to mix those up. He also
8

explained that _____ stands for pint and _____ stands for quart. Finally, he pointed out that
9   10

_____ stands for pound and _____ stands for ounce. The assistant thought it was confusing
11   12

but promised to learn the abbreviations.

undercooked	undercharged	underpaid	undersized

The new restaurant was terrible! The dining room is _____, so it was very
13

crowded. I ordered chicken, and it was _____. I had to send it back. I think all
14

of the staff must be _____. They weren't interested in working very hard. And
15

I think the waitress has trouble with math. She _____ us. After we corrected
16

the bill, we left and promised ourselves to never come back.

Grocery Stores and Supermarkets

In this lesson, you will work with words about grocery stores and supermarkets. Read this conversation between two roommates, Susan and Ann.

Susan: Ann, I'm going to Ted's Grocery Store. Do you need anything?

Ann: Ted's Grocery? Do you still shop there? I shop at Superfoods Supermarket. Why do you shop at Ted's?

Susan: I know that Ted's is small, but it's **convenient.** I can get everything I need there.

Ann: But the **selection** at Superfoods is so much better! For example, the **deli** in Ted's Grocery Store has only one **brand** of turkey. At Superfoods I can choose from five brands.

Susan: Well, I only buy one brand, so Ted's is fine with me.

Ann: What about all of the other departments? Superfoods has a great **bakery,** a full-service pharmacy, a floral department, a fresh seafood section, and a huge **produce** section. The **shelves** at Superfoods are **stocked** with every product you could ever need. And there's even an ATM if you need some cash.

Susan: That sounds great, but Superfoods is just too big for me. I get tired just pushing the **cart** up and down all of those **aisles!** If it's OK with you, I'll just keep shopping at Ted's for my **groceries.** I can go to the drugstore, the florist, and the seafood market on my way home from work to pick up what I need at those places.

Susan: Have it your way.

Ann: So, you didn't answer my question. Do you need anything from Ted's?

Susan: Well, actually, I do. Could you buy a **package** of hamburger rolls for me?

Exercise 1

Definitions
Write each word or phrase next to its definition.

aisle	cart	groceries	selection
bakery	convenient	package	shelf
brand	deli	produce	stock

_____ 1. fruits and vegetables

_____ 2. to fill a shelf with items for sale

_____ 3. a large basket with four wheels that you can push around a store

_____ 4. a place where baked goods such as bread, cookies, and cakes are made and sold

_____ 5. easy to use because it does not waste time or cause problems

_____ 6. a thin, flat piece of wood or metal that is used to hold items in a store

_____ 7. food and other supplies for the home that people buy at a store

_____ 8. a group of items that are wrapped together

_____ 9. short for "delicatessen," a shop or supermarket department that sells cooked meats, cheeses, and other ready-to-eat foods

_____ 10. an open space to walk between rows of shelves

_____ 11. a collection of items for sale from which things may be chosen

_____ 12. a category of products with a particular name, made by one company

Abbreviations

Match the abbreviation with the word
or words that it represents.

> When you shop at a grocery store or read an ad in the newspaper, you often see abbreviations. When you read an abbreviation, you say the whole word. For example, when you read *mgr.,* you say *manager.*

_____ 1. dept.   a. large

_____ 2. pkg.   b. department

_____ 3. ea.   c. manager

_____ 4. dz.   d. dozen

_____ 5. mgr.   e. medium

_____ 6. asst. mgr.   f. assistant manager

_____ 7. lg.   g. each

_____ 8. med.   h. package

Compound Words

Choose a word from each box. Combine
the words into a compound word and
write the new word on the line.

> Compound words are words made up of two or more words. Each is written as one word and has a special meaning that comes from the combination of words.

blue	drug	home	sea
card	every	near	tooth

berries	by	made	store
board	food	paste	thing

1. We found a _____ box behind the supermarket.

2. Do you buy _____ at the supermarket, or do you buy it at the drugstore?

3. The produce department sells fresh _____.

4. I like Ted's Grocery Store because it is _____.

5. She can get _____ she needs there.

6. The supermarket doesn't have a _____ department, so I go to a fish market.

7. I get my prescriptions filled in the pharmacy at my local _____.

8. The deli sells potato salad that tastes _____.

Prefix

> The prefix *super–* can mean *larger or better than other things or people of a similar type.*

Choose a word from the box, add *super–* to it, and write it on the line.

computer	human	market	powers
heroes	man	model	star

1. He acts in movies and on TV, and he sings. I think he is a _____.

2. The big company uses a _____, which is much more powerful than the one on your desk.

3. That beautiful woman looks like a _____ I saw on TV.

4. The U.S. and some other countries are considered _____.

5. Batman and Spiderman are _____.

6. Some movie characters are very strong. They have _____ strength.

7. When Clark Kent changes his clothes, he becomes _____.

8. I get all of my groceries from the _____ near the highway.

Suffix

> The suffix *–er* changes an adjective to the comparative form, meaning *more.*

Choose an adjective from the box, add *–er* to it, and write it on the line. Note: If an adjective ends with *–e,* you drop the *–e* and add *–er.*

cheap	fast	large	new
clean	fresh	neat	nice

1. Ann thinks Ted's is expensive. Superfoods is _____.

2. She thinks Ted's is too old. Superfoods is _____.

3. Ted's is too small. Superfoods is _____.

4. Ted's floors are dirty. Superfoods' floors are _____.

5. The cashiers at Ted's are unfriendly. At Superfoods they are _____.

6. Sometimes the aisles at Ted's are messy. The aisles at Superfoods are _____.

7. The bread at Ted's is stale. Superfoods' bread is _____.

8. The service at Ted's is too slow. The service at Superfoods is _____.

Antonyms

Choose an antonym from the box for each underlined word and write it on the line.

dirty	enormous	fresh	polite
empty	expensive	old-fashioned	speedy

1. That store sells <u>stale</u> bread at half price, but I only buy _____ bread.

2. Sometimes I choose the _____ product, since <u>cheaper</u> isn't always better.

3. Do you prefer a <u>modern</u> supermarket or an _____ grocery store?

4. The supermarket has an _____ parking lot, and the deli has a <u>tiny</u> one.

5. I thought that the bakery looked _____. I want to buy my bread from a <u>clean</u> place.

6. The service in the meat department is _____, but the checkout lines are <u>slow</u>.

7. They stocked the _____ shelves overnight, so now they are all <u>full</u>.

8. Cashiers have to be _____, even when customers are <u>rude</u> to them.

Collocations

We use many two-word collocations when we talk about people, places, and things in a grocery store.

Choose a word from the box and write it on the line.

aisle	carts	lot	name
card	coupons	manager	register

1. I found the breakfast food in the cereal _____.

2. The produce _____ had to stock more oranges.

3. Brand _____ items often cost more.

4. You can pay with your credit _____.

5. Hand your discount _____ to the cashier.

6. You can leave your cart in the parking _____.

7. At the end of the day, there is a lot of money in the cash _____.

8. Most shopping _____ have a place where a young child can sit.

Confusing Words

Circle the word that best completes
each sentence.

> Some common words that we use to talk about a grocery store have homophones. Homophones are words that are pronounced the same but have different spellings and different meanings.

1. I saw an (ad/add) in the newspaper that told about the special prices.

2. That supermarket is going to (hire/higher) a new cashier.

3. I bought (ate/eight) bottles of soda.

4. Sometimes, if you buy one item you get the second for one (cent/sent).

5. You can buy one candy bar or a (hole/whole) box.

6. The (pairs/pears) they have in the produce section look delicious.

7. I found the syrup in the cereal (isle/aisle).

8. Tomato sauce is on (sail/sale) this week.

9. The (cereal/serial) numbers on the box are 34587 and 34588.

10. If you come to customer service, you can (meat/meet) the manager.

11. I need to stop (by/buy) the drugstore on my way home.

12. I like Frank and Ed's because (their/there) meat is always fresh.

13. The bag had a (hole/whole) in it and the flour spilled on the floor.

14. They put the candy (hire/higher) on the shelf so the children can't reach it.

15. I picked up an extra item, so the cashier needs to (ad/add) it to my bill.

16. I don't like Ted's market because the (meat/meet) is too expensive.

17. Some breakfast (cereal/serial) has too much sugar in it.

18. I think Superfoods is too big, so I don't shop (their/there).

19. When I was six years old, my mother (cent/sent) me to the store for milk.

20. If you are going to bake bread, you will need to buy (flour/flower).

21. They (ate/eight) all of the pears, so we need to buy more.

22. I need to buy a new (pear/pair) of scissors for my kitchen.

Context Clues

Choose a word or phrase from below
each line and write it on the line.

1. I usually buy the store _____ since the products that you see
   brand / price / cart
   advertised on television are usually more expensive.

2. I think Ted's is very _____. I can stop on my way home from
   expensive / old-fashioned / convenient
   work, it's easy to park there, and it has everything I need.

3. If you are going to buy a lot, be sure you get a shopping _____
   coupon / cash register / cart
   on your way into the store.

4. I need to stop by the _____ to buy some sliced meats and
   produce department / deli / cereal aisle
   cheese for sandwiches.

5. I didn't find the pasta where I was looking, so I turned around and looked on another
   _____.
   shelf / cart / coupon

6. August is a good month to find fresh _____ in the produce
   blueberries / chicken / seafood
   department.

7. I don't shop at that little grocery store because its _____ isn't
   convenient / selection / shelf
   good enough.

8. My supermarket always has fresh _____. Yesterday I bought
   seafood / produce / deli
   salmon and clams.

Parts of Speech

Identify the underlined words. Write *N*
on the line if the word is a noun, and
write *V* if it is a verb.

> **Many common vocabulary words that end in –s can
> work either as plural nouns or as third-person singular
> verbs. Look for a noun after a preposition, and look for a
> verb after *he, she,* or *it.***

_____ 1. Mr. Smith buys extra groceries. He <u>stores</u> them in his house.

_____ 2. He takes a lot of <u>orders</u> over the phone.

_____ 3. There is a special place in the parking lot for <u>carts</u>.

_____ 4. The manager makes phone calls. He <u>orders</u> groceries from the warehouse.

_____ 5. The cashier has a special spot in her drawer for <u>checks</u>.

_____ 6. The clerk works at night. She <u>checks</u> the shelves and stocks the items.

_____ 7. That truck comes once a day. It <u>carts</u> away the garbage.

_____ 8. There are dozens of <u>stores</u> in that shopping center.

Dictionary

Identify the part of speech of each underlined word. Write *N, V,* or *Adj.*
on the line. Then look up the word in your dictionary. Choose and
write the best definition.

_____ 1. I only shop at markets where the seafood is <u>fresh</u>.

  definition: _____

_____ 2. He <u>stores</u> the extra groceries in the stockroom.

  definition: _____

_____ 3. I don't shop at places where the <u>service</u> is slow.

  definition: _____

_____ 4. They <u>package</u> children's cereal in colorful boxes.

  definition: _____

_____ 5. They shouldn't <u>market</u> candy to children.

  definition: _____

Crossword Puzzle

Fill in the puzzle with words from the box.

aisle	cardboard	Ea.	homemade	produce	shopping
blueberries	deli	enormous	modern	selection	stocks
brand	Dept.	groceries	Pkg.	shelves	supermarket

ACROSS

2. After a busy day, the _____ are almost empty.
3. The clerk _____ the shelves every night.
7. The opposite of *old-fashioned* is _____.
8. They store the products in _____ boxes.
9. You can get breakfast foods in the cereal _____.
10. _____ is the abbreviation for *package*.
11. _____ is the abbreviation for *each*.
12. A big supermarket has a better _____ than a little grocery store.
15. You can buy _____ in the produce section.
16. _____ is the abbreviation for *department*.

DOWN

1. They sell _____ salads in the deli.
2. I buy everything I need in a large _____.
4. There's a place in front of the store for _____ carts.
5. I buy all of my _____ in a large supermarket.
6. Another word for *very large* is _____.
10. They sell three kinds of tomatoes in the _____ section.
13. You will spend more money if you only buy _____ names.
14. You can buy sliced cheese in the _____.

Vocabulary in Context

Choose a word from the box and write it on the line.

| clean | empty | fresh | modern | speedy | tiny |

I love the new supermarket in my neighborhood. I'll never go back to the old store. The new

place is _____, but the old place was dirty. The new place has an enormous

1

parking lot and full shelves, while the old place had a _____ parking lot and

2

_____ shelves. The old place often sold stale bread, but my new store only

3

sells _____ bread. I also love the _____ service at the new

4   5

place. I like that much better than the slow service at my old store. I definitely prefer

_____ over old-fashioned.

6

| convenient | drugstore | everything | nearby | parking | seafood |

I love my _____ neighborhood. I shop at a _____ shopping

7   8

center, where I can buy _____ I need. If they don't have what I need in the

9

supermarket, I can go to other stores. If I need toothpaste, I can go to a _____.

10

If I need _____, I can go to a fish market. I just leave my car in one

11

_____ lot and walk from store to store.

12

| aisle | bakery | deli | produce | register | shelf |

Four friends went to a supermarket. Alice got bread at the _____. Beth got

13

apples in the _____ department. Cathy got sliced turkey at the

14

_____. Debbie took some chips off the _____ in the snack

15   16

food _____. Then they met at the cash _____.

17   18

The Weather

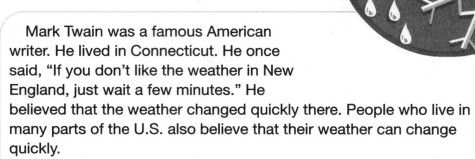

In this lesson, you will work with words about the weather. Read this story about the weather where Miriam lives.

Mark Twain was a famous American writer. He lived in Connecticut. He once said, "If you don't like the weather in New England, just wait a few minutes." He believed that the weather changed quickly there. People who live in many parts of the U.S. also believe that their weather can change quickly.

Miriam lives in Virginia. The weather can change very quickly there, too. Miriam remembers a day last winter. The sun was shining in the morning. It was warm. Miriam wore a sweater instead of a coat. That was a mistake. It snowed in the afternoon! After that Miriam learned to check the weather **forecast** before deciding what to wear.

Even with the changeable weather, Miriam likes the **climate** in Virginia. Sometimes the winters are **mild**. And there are many sunny days in the summer. Spring can be **chilly** and **damp**, but the fall is generally dry and cool. The **frost** on the ground on a fall morning is very beautiful. Usually, the weather in Virginia is pretty nice.

Sometimes, however, Virginia has **severe** weather. One winter a couple of years ago, there was a **blizzard**. Miriam couldn't go outside for three days. Later that year, a big **thunderstorm** produced **hail**. Miriam's car was damaged, but she thought she was pretty lucky. She heard about a **tornado** that touched down nearby. And in the early fall last year a **hurricane** hit the coast of Virginia, near Virginia Beach. Miriam experienced a lot of weather in a few short years.

Definitions

Write each word next to its definition.

blizzard	damp	hail	severe
chilly	forecast	hurricane	thunderstorm
climate	frost	mild	tornado

_____ 1. humid

_____ 2. the usual weather in a place

_____ 3. round pieces of frozen rain that fall from the sky

_____ 4. a violent storm in which it snows heavily and the wind blows for several hours

_____ 5. a storm that is common in warm weather that results from strong rising air currents and produces lightning

_____ 6. a thin white covering of ice that forms when moisture in the air freezes on the cold ground

_____ 7. a storm that develops over water that has high winds and produces a lot of rain; the winds blow in a large spiral around the center of the storm

_____ 8. a rotating column of air in the shape of a funnel, usually produced by a thunderstorm

_____ 9. a prediction about how something like the weather will be in the future

_____ 10. cool enough to make one feel uncomfortable

_____ 11. extremely bad or dangerous

_____ 12. not too cold or wet

Exercise 2

Abbreviations

Match the abbreviation with the word or words that it represents.

> When you read a weather forecast in a newspaper, you often see abbreviations. When you read an abbreviation, you say the whole word. For example, when you read *temp.* you say *temperature.*

_____ 1. min.   a. maximum

_____ 2. F   b. ultra-violet

_____ 3. UV   c. average

_____ 4. temp.   d. inch

_____ 5. mph   e. Fahrenheit

_____ 6. in.   f. temperature

_____ 7. max.   g. miles per hour

_____ 8. avg.   h. minimum

Exercise 3

Compound Words

Choose a word from each box. Combine the words into a compound word and write the new word on the line.

> Compound words are words made up of two or more words. Each is written as one word and has a special meaning that comes from the combination of words.

day	north	snow	thunder
drive	rain	sun	weather

ball	light	shine	way
drops	man	storm	west

1. My favorite _____ is on the television now.

2. That severe _____ produced high winds and hail.

3. The winds are _____ at 5 mph.

4. Tomorrow's forecast is for blue skies and _____.

5. When it stops snowing, we can have a _____ fight.

6. We cancelled the picnic after we saw _____ on the sidewalk.

7. He shoveled the snow out of the _____ after the blizzard.

8. In September, we have equal amounts of _____ and darkness.

Prefix

> The prefix *fore–* can mean *before,* or it can mean *the front part of something.*

Decide which meaning *fore–* has in each
sentence. Write *before* or *front* on the line.

_____ 1. I watch the weather <u>fore</u>cast every night.

_____ 2. My <u>fore</u>arms hurt from shoveling snow.

_____ 3. The raindrop hit me on the <u>fore</u>head.

_____ 4. Is it possible to <u>fore</u>see next year's weather?

_____ 5. They <u>fore</u>warned the people about the tornado.

_____ 6. There are flowers in the <u>fore</u>ground of the picture.

_____ 7. A camping trip requires a lot of <u>fore</u>thought.

_____ 8. I don't think I'll go in the <u>fore</u>seeable future.

Exercise 5: Word Builder

Suffix

> The suffix *–est* changes an adjective to the superlative form, meaning *most.*

Study the spelling rules. Then choose an
adjective from the box, add *–est* to it, and write it on the line.

> **Rule 1:** If an adjective is one syllable, has one vowel, and ends
> with one consonant, then double the consonant before
> you add *–est.*
> **Rule 2:** If an adjective ends with a consonant followed by *–y,*
> change the *–y* to *–i* and add *–est.*

| chilly | early | rainy | wet |
| dry | hot | sunny | windy |

1. Seattle has the most rainfall. It's the _____ city.

2. The sun shines a lot in Miami. It's the _____ city.

3. Florida's temperatures are high. It's the _____ state.

4. It is really wet in March. March is the _____ month.

5. It never rains in the desert. That is the _____ place.

6. The wind blows in Chicago. That's the _____ city.

7. April is cool and rainy. That's the _____ month.

8. It snowed in September! It was the _____ snowfall ever.

Antonyms

Choose an antonym from the box for each underlined word and write it on the line.

cloudy	freezes	lightly	warm
earlier	humid	rises	windy

1. I have a friend who loves _____ days and hates <u>sunny</u> days.

2. Florida's weather is very _____, while Arizona has a lot of <u>dry</u> days.

3. Some days in April are _____, but other days are <u>chilly</u>.

4. The lake _____ in December and <u>thaws</u> in May.

5. We can't sail the boat when it's too _____ or when it's too <u>calm</u>.

6. The water level _____ and <u>falls</u> with the tides.

7. The sun rises _____ in the summer and <u>later</u> in the winter.

8. If it's raining _____, we can go. Let's not go if it's raining too <u>hard</u>.

Collocations

Choose a word from the box and write it on the line.

We use many two-word collocations when we talk about weather conditions. Some of them contain *and* or *or.*

dense	night	rain	thunder
hot	partly	sleet	

1. I'm afraid of _____ and lightning.

2. The weather doesn't matter. We'll have the picnic _____ or shine.

3. It snowed day and _____ during the blizzard.

4. Tomorrow's forecast is for _____ cloudy skies.

5. The airport was closed due to _____ fog.

6. Winter storms often contain snow and _____.

7. Summer weather is often _____ and humid.

Confusing Words

Circle the words that best complete
each sentence.

> *A little* and *a few* are both quantifiers. Use *a little* before a noncount noun. Noncount nouns are never plural. Use *a few* before a countable noun that is plural.

1. There were (a little/a few) thunderstorms last week.

2. At the beginning of the storm, I even saw (a little/a few) hail.

3. There wasn't much rain. I saw (a little/a few) raindrops on the sidewalk.

4. It was a beautiful day. There were only (a little/a few) clouds in the sky.

5. The weather in Georgia is mild, but some parts of the state get (a little/a few) snow in the winter.

6. When I was in San Francisco, I saw only (a little/a few) fog.

7. They say it rains a lot in Seattle, but I saw (a little/a few) sunshine there.

8. States like Montana have (a little/a few) tornadoes every year.

Circle the words that best complete
each sentence.

> *Too much* and *too many* both tell about an excessive amount, an amount that is unacceptable to the speaker. Use *too much* before a noncount noun. Noncount nouns are never plural. Use *too many* before a countable noun that is plural.

9. I couldn't see the moon because there were (too much/too many) clouds.

10. People feel uncomfortable when there is (too much/too many) humidity.

11. We couldn't drive because there was (too much/too many) ice on the road.

12. Our vacation was pretty good, except there were (too much/too many) thunderstorms.

13. I think there are (too much/too many) tornadoes in Kansas.

14. We couldn't have our picnic because there was (too much/too many) wind.

15. I'm confused because I heard (too much/too many) different forecasts.

16. I think there are (too much/too many) hurricanes in Florida.

Context Clues

Choose a word from below each
line and write it on the line.

It is often possible to guess a missing word from the
context of a sentence. When you rely on context, you
use what you know about the other words in the
sentence to help you guess the word.

1. Be sure to take a hat, sunglasses, and sunscreen on your vacation, because there is a lot

   of _____ in Florida.
   rain / sunshine / fog

2. Yesterday afternoon the temperature was pleasant, but I put on a sweater last night

   because the air felt _____.
   chilly / warm / dry

3. Last winter, the weather was very mild. We didn't have any _____
   chilly / severe / warm

   weather like blizzards or ice storms.

4. I know that it is still winter, but don't go ice skating on the lake. The ice isn't thick enough.

   The weather has been warm, and the lake is starting to _____.
   freeze / dry / thaw

5. She bought a snow shovel, a flashlight, and enough food for three days after the weather

   forecast predicted a _____.
   blizzard / thunderstorm / tornado

6. It was a terrible storm! The _____ as big as golf balls made
   Raindrops / Hail / Clouds

   dents in my car!

7. One morning last fall, there was a thin layer of white _____ on
   lightning / wind / frost

   the ground when we woke up.

8. It was so _____ that my hat blew right off my head.
   windy / sunny / humid

Parts of Speech

Identify the underlined words. Write *Adj.* on the line if the word is an adjective, and write *Adv.* if it is an adverb.

> Adjectives modify nouns, and adverbs usually modify action verbs. You can usually make an adverb from an adjective by adding *–ly,* but some words use the same word for both forms. Four of these words that work as both adjectives and adverbs are *early, hard, hourly,* and *straight.* Look for an adjective before a noun or after *be.* Look for an adverb after an action verb.

_____ 1. The forecast changed <u>hourly</u>.

_____ 2. The rain fell <u>straight</u> down, so it didn't come in my window.

_____ 3. We were happy to see the spring after a <u>hard</u> winter.

_____ 4. The snow began falling <u>early</u>.

_____ 5. I turn on my radio for an <u>hourly</u> update about the weather.

_____ 6. She shoveled a <u>straight</u> path from her front door to her driveway.

_____ 7. It snowed <u>hard</u> for three days.

_____ 8. The September storm brought an <u>early</u> snow.

Dictionary

Identify the part of speech of each underlined word. Write *V, Adj.,* or *Adv.* on the line. Then look up the word in your dictionary. Choose and write the best definition.

_____ 1. We had a very <u>hard</u> winter.

definition: _____

_____ 2. It rained for three days <u>straight</u>.

definition: _____

_____ 3. Tom got angry and <u>stormed</u> out of the room.

definition: _____

_____ 4. If your skin gets dry in the winter, use a <u>mild</u> soap.

definition: _____

_____ 5. If you don't want to walk in the rain, you can <u>hail</u> a taxi.

definition: _____

Crossword Puzzle

Fill in the puzzle with words from the box.

avg.	forecast	hail	rainiest	straight	thaw
blizzard	foresee	humid	rises	sunshine	weatherman
earliest	forewarned	partly	snowman	temp.	windiest

ACROSS

1. Is April the _____ month?
6. We built a _____ after the snow stopped falling.
7. Summer weather is often hot and _____.
8. The _____ forecasted the storm.
13. Is March the _____ month?
16. The abbreviation for *average* is _____.
17. The _____ snow comes in October.
18. Tomorrow will be _____ cloudy.

DOWN

2. It rained for four days _____.
3. I watched the weather _____ on television.
4. The people went to the basement when they were _____ about the tornado.
5. We have the most _____ on clear days.
9. They didn't _____ the storm. It was a surprise.
10. Two feet of snow fell during the _____.
11. The temperature sometimes _____ to 100 degrees in the summer.
12. The lake begins to _____ in March.
14. The abbreviation for *temperature* is _____.
15. Sometimes thunderstorms produce _____.

Vocabulary in Context
Choose a word from the box and write it on the line.

climate	damp	frost	hard	mild	severe	tornado

Fred hates the _____ where he lives. The weather in the spring is always
1
_____ and very cool. In the summer, there are _____
2   3
thunderstorms every afternoon. Last summer there was even a _____. Then,
4
in the fall, there is _____ on the ground by the first of October. The winters
5
are always _____. Fred is ready to move to a place with a
6
_____ climate.
7

driveway	humid	northwest	raindrops
hail	lightning	partly	thunderstorm

Yesterday, there was a severe _____ in Fred's neighborhood. The weather
8
was very hot and _____, and it was _____ cloudy in the
9   10
morning. Fred was outside in the later afternoon, and he noticed some dark clouds in the
_____. Then there were a few _____ on his
11   12
_____. Then, all of a sudden, Fred saw a flash of _____. He
13   14
ran into the garage just before it started to _____.
15

avg.	F	max.	temp.	UV

I have to remember what the abbreviations mean when I read about the weather. It's easy to
remember that _____ stands for *temperature,* and _____
16   17
stands for *average.* I have trouble remembering that _____ means *Fahrenheit,*
18
and that _____ means *ultra-violet.* I know that _____ stands
19   20
for *maximum,* but when I read *min.,* I'm not sure if it means *minimum* or *minute.*

Job Hunting

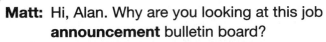

In this lesson, you will work with words about finding a job. Read this conversation between two friends, Matt and Alan.

Matt: Hi, Alan. Why are you looking at this job **announcement** bulletin board?

Alan: Oh, hi, Matt. Well, because I'm looking for a job.

Matt: I thought you were going to get a job as a **mechanic**.

Alan: Yes, I hope to do that, but first I have to finish my **certificate** in automotive light repair at the community college.

Matt: Oh, I see. So which job are you going to apply for?

Alan: I'm not sure. I need a job that doesn't require special **skills** or **training**.

Matt: That might be difficult. What **experience** do you have?

Alan: I worked as a supermarket cashier and a nursing home **aide**.

Matt: I think you have good **qualifications** for a lot of these jobs.

Alan: Really?

Matt: Sure. Look, I think you could apply for this job as a deli clerk. You already have supermarket experience. Or how about a job as a nursing home **receptionist?** You know how to answer telephones.

Alan: Yes, those look like good possibilities.

Matt: The ad from the nursing home says you need a high school **diploma**. Did you graduate from high school?

Alan: No, I didn't, but I got my GED last year.

Matt: Oh, that's great.

Alan: Do you know how I can get an **application** form for these jobs?

Matt: I think you call the number on the announcement.

Alan: Ah, yes, I see that now. Thanks a lot for the advice.

Matt: You're welcome, and good luck with your job **search!**

Definitions

Write each word next to its definition.

aide	certificate	mechanic	search
announcement	diploma	qualification	skill
application	experience	receptionist	training

_____ 1. instruction or teaching that leads to learning a skill

_____ 2. a document that you receive when you complete a short course of study to show that you have the necessary training to do a job

_____ 3. a person whose job is to answer telephones and greet visitors

_____ 4. a public message that is posted, printed, or broadcast to let people know that something is available or going to happen

_____ 5. knowledge, skills, or understanding that you gain from doing an activity or job

_____ 6. a worker who is skilled in repairing motors and machines

_____ 7. a quality or accomplishment that makes a person able or fit to do a particular job or task

_____ 8. the action of looking for something carefully

_____ 9. the ability to do something well, especially after training or practice

_____ 10. a person whose job is to help another person; an assistant

_____ 11. a document that you receive when you graduate from high school or college to show that you have successfully completed the course of study

_____ 12. a written request for employment

Initializations

Match each initialization with the words
or term that it represents.

Many job announcements and job applications use sets
of initials to refer to a variety of concepts. You can explain
these initializations with sentences using *stands for.*

_____ 1. HR   a. not applicable

_____ 2. PT   b. General Educational Development

_____ 3. FT   c. part-time

_____ 4. NA   d. human resources

_____ 5. EOE   e. commercial driver's license

_____ 6. GED   f. as soon as possible

_____ 7. CDL   g. Equal Opportunity Employer

_____ 8. ASAP   h. full-time

Compound Words

Choose a word from each box. Combine
the words into a compound word and
write the new word on the line.

Compound words are words made up of two or more
words. Each is written as one word and has a special
meaning that comes from the combination of words.
Many job titles are compound words.

bar	fire	house	police
dish	hair	life	sales

dresser	guard	man	tender
fighter	keeper	person	washer

1. The _____ drives a patrol car.

2. The _____ gets a commission on everything he or she sells.

3. The _____ works on several floors of the hotel.

4. The _____ has his or her hands in hot water all evening.

5. The _____ rides to emergencies on a truck.

6. The _____ watches people swim.

7. The _____ washes, cuts, dries, straightens, curls, and colors.

8. The _____ mixes drinks until the restaurant closes.

Exercise 4: Word Builder

Prefix

Choose a verb from the box, add *out–* to it, and write it on the line.

The prefix *out–* can mean *bigger, greater, farther,* or *more* when you add it to a verb.

bid	number	run	shine
live	ranks	sell	weigh

1. The car salesperson wants to _____ all the other salespeople at the dealership.

2. Your boss _____ you.

3. If the sons _____ their father, they will own the company.

4. Some qualifications are more important, so they _____ the others.

5. The workers _____ the supervisors by about 10 to 1.

6. The company didn't get the contract because another company _____ them.

7. The soccer player can _____ the baseball player any day.

8. If you want the job, you have to _____ all of the other people who apply.

Exercise 5: Word Builder

Suffix

Choose a noun from the box and write it on the line.

The suffix *–ant* indicates that a word is a noun, often a person who does something.

accountant	assistant	consultant	servant
applicants	attendant	contestant	

1. The executive hired an _____ to help her.

2. A _____ usually gives professional advice.

3. I had a job as an _____, working on financial records.

4. Look for a job as a flight _____ if you like to travel.

5. They asked all of the _____ to come for interviews.

6. He wants to be a public _____ and work for the government.

7. You can't find a job as a game show _____.

Synonyms

Choose a word from the box that means about the same as each underlined word or phrase. Write the word on the line.

assistant	employee	factory	supervisor
assists	experience	mall	training

1. The nursing home aide _____ the patients and <u>helps</u> the nurses.

2. They are hiring clerks in the _____ and in the other <u>shopping center</u>.

3. Talk to the _____ about your application, since he will be your <u>boss</u>.

4. I worked in a _____ before, so I hope to get a job in an automobile <u>plant</u>.

5. I was an _____ in a preschool, so maybe I can be a kindergarten <u>aide</u>.

6. I need more _____ because they only hire people with sufficient <u>education</u>.

7. Read the _____ handbook if you want to know about your rights as a <u>worker</u>.

8. If you have the right <u>knowledge</u> and _____, you will get the job.

Collocations

We use many two-word collocations when we talk about job titles.

Choose a word from the box and write it on the line.

aide	driver	officer	server
carrier	guard	processor	teller

1. If you are good with numbers, you can be a bank _____.

2. If you like working with sick people, you can be a nurse's _____.

3. You can be a mail _____ if you don't mind walking.

4. If you have your CDL, you can be a truck _____.

5. To be a police _____, you have to graduate from the academy.

6. If you work in the cafeteria, you can be a food _____.

7. If you are a security _____, you have to wear a uniform.

8. If you are good at typing, you could be a word _____.

Confusing Words

Complete each sentence with *advice* or *advise*.

> *Advice* and *advise* are often confused. *Advice* is a noun. *Advise* is a verb.

1. Can you _____ me on getting a job?

2. What _____ do you have on job hunting?

3. I read some _____ about job interviews.

4. When will you _____ me?

5. I have _____ for you about the interview.

6. The job counselors _____ people about their applications.

7. How much _____ did they give you?

8. What did they _____ you to do?

Circle the word that best completes each sentence.

> *Advice* is a noncount noun, and it is never plural. If you want to talk about more than one piece of advice, you can use the word *recommendations*.

9. The advisor gave me several useful (advice/recommendations).

10. How much of her (advice/recommendations) did you use?

11. I think Matt gave Alan a couple of good (advice/recommendations).

12. Only two of her (advice/recommendations) were useful.

13. Before your interview, you should ask for a little (advice/recommendations).

14. You want to help your friend, but don't give her too many (advice/recommendations).

15. I think Alan wanted a little (advice/recommendations) from Matt.

16. He didn't offer too much (advice/recommendations).

17. How many of the (advice/recommendations) were good ones?

18. (Advice/Recommendations) are not always useful.

Context Clues

Choose a word from below each
line and write it on the line.

1. I read all of the job _____ that were posted on the board and
   announcements / diplomas / aides
   listed in the newspaper. I couldn't find one job that I wanted to apply for.

2. I didn't get the job. Even though I had the training, I didn't have enough

   _____ doing that type of work in my previous employment.
   training / applications / experience

3. That's an interesting job. But do you have the right _____ to
   qualifications / announcements / searches
   do it?

4. He got a job as a _____. Now he works mixing drinks four
   dishwasher / hairdresser / bartender
   nights a week in a restaurant. The pay is low but the tips are good.

5. If the applicants _____ the positions, then some people won't get
   outlive / outnumber / outrank
   jobs. In other words, if there are 10 positions and 20 applicants, then 10 people won't get jobs.

6. I'm looking for a new job. Right now, I'm a _____ in a busy
   salesperson / bartender / dishwasher
   restaurant. I don't like having my hands in hot water for several hours a night.

7. I have some experience working with elderly people. I was a _____
   nurse's aide / bank teller / police officer
   in a nursing home for two years.

8. I went to the community college and got a/an _____ in computer-
   application / certificate / supervisor
   aided design. I completed five classes. Now I can look for a job in an engineering office.

Parts of Speech

Identify the underlined words. Write *V*
on the line if the word is a verb, and write
Adj. if it is an adjective.

Many common vocabulary words that end in *–ed* can
work either as verbs or as adjectives. Look for a verb
after a subject and before an object. Look for an
adjective before a noun.

_____ 1. The human resources department made a list of <u>qualified</u> candidates.

_____ 2. The school <u>educated</u> him, but the workplace trained him to do the job.

_____ 3. They only hire <u>experienced</u> drivers to drive school buses.

_____ 4. They need <u>trained</u> drivers who have their CDLs.

_____ 5. He thought working in the nursing home <u>qualified</u> him to work in a hospital, too.

_____ 6. An <u>educated</u> person finds it easy to get jobs.

_____ 7. The bartending school <u>trained</u> us well.

_____ 8. She <u>experienced</u> some difficult moments in her last job.

Dictionary

Identify the part of speech of each underlined word. Write *N, V,* or *Adj.*
on the line. Then look up the word in your dictionary. Choose and
write the best definition.

_____ 1. Alan <u>experienced</u> a lot of problems in his last job.

    definition: _____

_____ 2. He lost his job at the steel <u>plant</u>.

    definition: _____

_____ 3. If you think you can do the job, I think you should <u>apply</u> for it.

    definition: _____

_____ 4. If you are not <u>qualified</u>, they won't hire you.

    definition: _____

_____ 5. He has worked with animals. He used to <u>train</u> dogs.

    definition: _____

Crossword Puzzle

Fill in the puzzle with words from the box.

aide	consultant	EOE	guard	outsells	search
ASAP	contestant	factory	hairdresser	outweigh	supervisor
certificate	diploma	FT	lifeguards	PT	teller

ACROSS

3. A player on a game show is a _____.
4. Your _____ is your boss.
8. _____ stands for *part-time*.
11. A _____ is like a plant.
12. They hire a lot of _____ in the summer.
14. If you see _____ in an announcement, it means *Equal Opportunity Employer*.
15. She got a job as a bank _____.
17. She worked as a nurse's _____ in a hospital.

DOWN

1. A _____ gives professional advice.
2. After graduation, the school sent my _____ in the mail.
3. He took courses and got a _____ in auto repair.
5. Some qualifications _____ others.
6. He worked as a security _____ at the plant.
7. The salesperson who _____ the others gets a bonus.
9. A _____ can get a job in a beauty salon.
10. _____ stands for *full-time*.
13. Good luck in your job _____!
16. If you have to send your application _____, that means do it as soon as possible.

Vocabulary in Context

Choose a word from the box and write it on the line.

> application   certificate   experience   mechanic   skills   training

Alan just completed his _____ in automotive maintenance. Now he is filling
                                    1
out an _____ for a job as a _____. He doesn't have very
                2   3
much _____, since he's never worked as a mechanic. But he hopes that his
                4
_____ at the college has given him the _____ that he needs.
            5   6

> bartender   firefighter   lifeguard   housekeeper   salesperson

Matt is trying to help Alan think of a job he could do. If he likes people, he could work in a bar

as a _____. Or if he likes selling things, he could be a _____.
                7   8
He knows you need special training to be a _____ and respond to emergency
                                                        9
calls, but perhaps if he likes dealing with emergencies, he could be a _____
                                                                                10
and work at a pool. Matt also knows that Alan's apartment is neat. Perhaps he could work in a

hotel as a _____.
                11

> carrier   driver   firefighter   guard   officer   training

Alan was thinking that he might like to work outside some of the time. He thought he might

like to be a mail _____, but there is a written exam for that job. Then he
                            12
thought about being a police _____ or a _____, but he
                                        13   14
realized he would need special _____ for those jobs. He decided to look into
                                            15
being a truck _____ or a security _____.
                        16   17

Sports

David and Greg are roommates. It's great that they live together, since they have so much in common. In fact, they are both huge sports **fans**. If you visit their apartment, you can be sure to find some kind of sports show on the television.

If you visit David and Greg in the summer, you can watch a baseball game with them. David will explain all of the **positions** to you and tell you how the **pitcher** and the **catcher** communicate. Greg will tell you about his favorite players, including the shortstop on his hometown team.

If you visit them in the fall, you'll see a football game with them. David will hope that you **root for** his hometown team and cheer when they make a **touchdown**.

David and Greg love to watch **professional** baseball and football, but when it comes to basketball they prefer to watch college teams play. March is their favorite basketball month because they get to watch "March Madness," the NCAA Basketball **Tournament**. When David and Greg's favorite teams are on the **court**, everything else in their lives stops.

You might think that all David and Greg do is watch television. That's not true. They play sports almost as much as they watch them. They both play on a local soccer team. David is the **goalie,** and Greg is a forward who plays left wing. When they are not on the soccer field, you might find them swimming at the pool, running at the track, skating at the ice **rink**, or **hiking** up a mountain.

Definitions

Write each word next to its definition.

catcher	goalie	position	root for
court	hiking	professional	touchdown
fan	pitcher	rink	tournament

_____ 1. to support a sports team by shouting and cheering

_____ 2. the baseball player who stays behind home plate to signal for and catch pitches

_____ 3. someone who likes a particular activity very much

_____ 4. extended walking for pleasure or exercise

_____ 5. the player who throws the baseball to the batter

_____ 6. a competition in which teams play a series of games to decide the winner

_____ 7. in sports, the area and action for which a player is responsible

_____ 8. an open area covered with smooth ice for skating or hockey

_____ 9. an open, flat area that is marked with lines where you can play a game such as basketball or tennis

_____ 10. in sports, the term that refers to teams in which the players are paid

_____ 11. the player who is assigned to protect the goal in soccer, hockey, and some other sports

_____ 12. in football, the act of carrying the ball across the opponent's goal line

Exercise 2

Initializations

Match each initialization with the words that it represents.

Many sports associations and companies are identified by sets of initials. You can explain these initializations with sentences using *stands for.*

_____ 1. ESPN   a. National Collegiate Athletic Association

_____ 2. NBA   b. National Hockey League

_____ 3. PGA   c. Major League Baseball

_____ 4. NCAA   d. National Football League

_____ 5. WNBA   e. Professional Golfers Association

_____ 6. NFL   f. Women's National Basketball Association

_____ 7. MLB   g. Entertainment and Sports Programming Network

_____ 8. NHL   h. National Basketball Association

Exercise 3

Compound Words

Choose a word from each box. Combine the words into a compound word and write the new word on the line.

Compound words are words made up of two or more words. Each is written as one word and has a special meaning that comes from the combination of words.

basket	home	quarter	short
goal	out	room	touch

back	down	keeper	stop
ball	field	mates	town

1. Greg grew up in New York, so he can root for several _____ teams.

2. In football, a team gets six points for a _____.

3. The NCAA regulates college _____.

4. The _____ is the player who calls the signals in the football game.

5. In baseball, the _____ plays between second and third base.

6. Greg and David are _____.

7. Another word for *goalie* is _____.

8. In baseball, three players play in the _____.

Exercise 4: Word Builder

Prefix

Circle the number prefix in each of the following and write the corresponding number on the line.

Several prefixes in English refer to numbers. For example, *uni–* means *one*, *bi–* means *two*, and *tri–* means *three*.

_____ 1. The players wear their blue uniforms when they play at home.

_____ 2. The best part of the baseball game was the triple play in the fourth inning.

_____ 3. Several baseball players from the Caribbean are bilingual.

_____ 4. He rode in a bicycle race.

_____ 5. In the triathlon, participants have to run, then swim, then bike.

_____ 6. He took binoculars to the stadium so he could see the players.

_____ 7. David's passion for football is not unique.

_____ 8. The players formed a triangle under the basket.

Exercise 5: Word Builder

Suffix

Study the spelling rules. Choose a verb from the box, add *–ing* to it, and write it on the line.

The suffix *–ing* changes a verb to a gerund. Use gerunds after *go* to talk about activities.

Rule 1: If a verb ends in *–e*, drop the *–e* before you add *–ing*.
Rule 2: If a verb ends with one vowel and one consonant, double the consonant before you add *–ing*.

bike	**jog**	**run**	**skate**
hike	**ride**	**shop**	**swim**

1. If you don't like to watch sports, you can go _____ at the mall on Sunday afternoons.

2. I'd like to go horseback _____.

3. In the winter you can go _____ at the ice rink.

4. If you can't run fast, you can go _____.

5. The marathon runner goes _____ every weekend.

6. We went _____ in the mountains and walked for five miles.

7. If you buy a bicycle, you can go _____ every weekend.

8. He likes to go _____ at the neighborhood pool in the summer.

Antonyms

Choose an antonym from the box for each underlined word and write it on the line.

> amateur   burning   freezes   national
> artificial   exciting   hits

1. Some people say soccer is _____ and baseball is <u>boring</u>.

2. Football players play in all conditions, from the _____ sun of Miami to the <u>freezing</u> wind of Minnesota.

3. Greg likes both <u>professional</u> and _____ sports.

4. If David can't watch a _____ game, he watches a <u>local</u> one.

5. Some stadiums have <u>natural</u> grass, but others use _____ turf.

6. You can go skating from the time the lake _____ until it <u>thaws</u>.

7. If the batter _____ the ball, he runs. If he <u>misses</u>, then it's a strike and he tries again.

Exercise 7

Collocations

Choose a word from the box and write it on the line.

> **We use many two-word collocations to talk about the places where sports are played.**

> baseball   hockey   soccer   tennis
> hiking   ski   swimming

1. The pitcher stands on a mound in the center of the _____ diamond.

2. They put up a new net at the _____ court in the park.

3. The goalie always stays at the end of the _____ field.

4. The team plays on an indoor _____ rink so the ice is always smooth.

5. They make artificial snow on the _____ slopes in those mountains.

6. Our _____ pool opens in May and closes in September.

7. The _____ trail on the mountain is covered in leaves in the fall.

Confusing Words

Study the use of these words. Then write
their, there, or *they're* on the line.

Their, there, and *they're* sound the same, but they are
used in different ways.

> *Their* is a possessive adjective that is used before a noun.
> *There* comes before a form of *be* to show that something exists.
> *There* is also used to mean *in that place.*
> *They're* is a contraction of *they* and *are.* It is used before
> adjectives, noun phrases, and verbs that end with *–ing.*

1. My favorite team lost _____ first game of the season.

2. I'm going to the park because the soccer game is _____.

3. I'm happy because my team is winning. _____ playing well.

4. _____ is a game on ESPN right now.

5. They have a great offense. _____ good at scoring this season.

6. Many fans wear _____ team's colors to games.

7. When the ticket office opened, I went _____ and got my season pass.

8. The game is starting. _____ running out onto the field now.

9. _____ are several ways to get out in baseball.

10. _____ is no chance that my team will win.

11. The football team is going to replace _____ quarterback.

12. They got _____ TV repaired before the tournament began.

13. _____ watching the NCAA Tournament now.

14. When I watch baseball, I don't understand what _____ doing in the outfield.

15. NCAA athletes are not professional. _____ amateur players.

16. They were selling hats in the parking lot, so I went _____ and bought one.

17. I don't know if _____ is a game on TV tonight.

18. The basketball players wear _____ blue uniforms when they play at home.

19. _____ better than they were last season.

20. Look in the newspaper for the scores. They are usually printed _____.

Context Clues

Choose a word from below each line
and write it on the line.

1. The team scored two touchdowns in the first quarter of the _____
   football / tennis / hockey
   game. The crowd in the stadium cheered.

2. The goalie prevented three goals in the first half of the _____ game.
   football / basketball / soccer

3. I think the _____ players must get tired from running up and
   baseball / basketball / football
   down the court the whole game.

4. I don't understand how the pitcher and the catcher communicate during the
   _____ game.
   baseball / basketball / football

5. A triathlon includes running, _____, and biking. If you want to
   hiking / jogging / swimming
   participate, you are going to have to get good running shoes, a bathing suit, and a bicycle.

6. As soon as the ice on the lake froze, we decided to go _____.
   skating / running / biking

7. After the catcher signals, the pitcher throws the _____ and the
   bat / ball / base
   catcher catches it.

8. The new soccer team wears green and white _____ since the
   uniforms / fans / courts
   team's colors are green and white.

Parts of Speech

Identify the underlined words. Write *N*
on the line if the word is a noun, and
write *V* if it is a verb.

Many words that we use when we talk about baseball
can work either as nouns or verbs. Look for a noun after
the or *a.* Look for a verb after *to.*

_____ 1. They couldn't play because the <u>field</u> was too wet.

_____ 2. Are you watching the game? What's the <u>score</u>?

_____ 3. Are they going to <u>play</u> in the rain?

_____ 4. Once you hit the ball, you have to <u>run</u>.

_____ 5. Let's watch that <u>play</u> again on the instant replay.

_____ 6. Young baseball players have to learn how to <u>field</u> the ball.

_____ 7. I think they are going to <u>score</u> another run.

_____ 8. They gave the player a "high five" after he scored the <u>run</u>.

Dictionary

Identify the part of speech of each underlined word. Write *N* or *V* on
the line. Then look up the word in your dictionary. Choose and write
the best definition.

_____ 1. I got a speeding ticket after the football game, so I had to go to <u>court</u>.

definition: _____

_____ 2. I <u>passed</u> the ball to Tom, and he scored the goal.

definition: _____

_____ 3. All of the players are going to <u>pool</u> their money to buy some new soccer balls.

definition: _____

_____ 4. The basketball player made five <u>fouls</u> and had to leave the game.

definition: _____

_____ 5. It's your turn to <u>bat</u> next. Be sure to watch the pitcher.

definition: _____

Crossword Puzzle

Fill in the puzzle with words from the box.

catcher	hometown	quarterback	stadium	tournament
diamond	NFL	rink	their	triathlon
ESPN	PGA	root for	There	uniforms
goalie	professional	score	touchdown	

ACROSS

1. If you _____ a team, you have to stand up and cheer.
4. They play both football and soccer in that _____.
8. The _____ signals to the pitcher and catches the ball.
11. The fans love _____ team.
12. We always root for our _____ team.
14. They watched the game on _____.
15. What is the _____?
16. They play hockey at the ice _____.
17. Only one team can win the _____.
19. _____ stands for *Professional Golfers Association*.

DOWN

2. A _____ combines three sports.
3. The _____ calls the signals in a football game.
5. The player carried the football across the goal line and made a _____.
6. The pitcher stands in the middle of the baseball _____.
7. _____ is always a game on ESPN.
9. The NBA is a _____ league.
10. They wear their white _____ for home games.
13. The _____ has to prevent the other team from scoring.
18. The _____ is the National Football League.

Vocabulary in Context

Choose a word from the box and write it on the line.

court	goalkeeper	position	quarterback	shortstop

Greg is not just a sports fan; he also plays several sports. Greg has his favorite

_____ in each sport. In baseball, Greg likes to play _____. On
1   2

the basketball _____, Greg likes to be a guard. On the soccer field, Greg is the
3

_____. And on the football team, Greg is a great _____.
4   5

biking	hiking	jogging	riding	running	skating	swimming

There are a lot of activities that you can do to stay healthy and fit. If you like to walk through

natural areas, you should try _____. If you like winter sports, you can go
6

_____. If you prefer to be more active in the summer, you can go
7

_____ at your local pool. If you have a lot of energy, you can go
8

_____ or _____. If you prefer to pedal for your exercise, you
9   10

can go _____, and if you really like animals you could try horseback
11

_____.
12

ESPN	NBA	NCAA	NHL	WNBA

David watches _____ every day. Yesterday, David watched two professional
13

basketball games, including one _____ game and one _____
14   15

game. He also watched an _____ hockey game and two
16

_____ college basketball games.
17

Shopping

In this lesson, you will work with words about shopping. Read this telephone conversation between two friends, Mary and Laura.

Mary: Hi, Laura. I'm going to the **mall** today. Would you like to go with me?

Laura: I thought you never shopped at the mall. Aren't you the one who likes to shop **downtown?**

Mary: Yes, I usually do, but last week I saw an **advertisement** about a sale at a department store in the mall. There was a **coupon** in the ad.

Laura: Oh, so you decided to break your rule and go to the mall.

Mary: Yes, I used the coupon and bought a dress. But now I don't like the dress, so I'm going to **return** it.

Laura: Didn't you **try** the dress **on** in the store?

Mary: I did, but the light in the **fitting room** wasn't bright enough, so I couldn't see how terrible the dress looks.

Laura: So are you going to exchange it?

Mary: If I find another dress that I like, I'll **exchange** it.

Laura: What if you don't find another dress?

Mary: I'll go to **customer service** and ask about getting a **refund**. I charged the dress on my credit card, so I don't know how they will handle the refund.

Laura: It sounds like you need help! I think I'll go with you.

Mary: Thanks. If I don't find another dress at the mall, maybe we can stop at the **discount** dress shop in the **shopping center** on the highway.

Laura: For a person who used to only shop downtown, you have a lot of options.

Mary: I guess I do! I'll pick you up in half an hour.

Definitions

Write each word or phrase next to its definition.

> advertisement   discount   fitting room   return
> coupon   downtown   mall   shopping center
> customer service   exchange   refund   try on

_____ 1. a place in a store equipped with mirrors where you can put on clothes to see if they are the right size and if they look good on you

_____ 2. a large indoor space containing shops and restaurants connected by passageways with benches where shoppers can rest

_____ 3. a place in a large store where you can get assistance with the store's products or services

_____ 4. describes a store where items are sold for a reduced price

_____ 5. to give something back where you bought it and to get a replacement

_____ 6. a picture and words, usually printed in a newspaper or magazine, telling people what they can buy or what is happening

_____ 7. to take something back to the store where you bought it because you are not satisfied with it

_____ 8. the main business and/or shopping area of a city or town

_____ 9. a group of stores sharing a common parking lot, often with easy access to a main road

_____ 10. a small printed piece of paper that gives a person a lower price on something

_____ 11. to put a piece of clothing on to see if it is the right size and/or if it looks good on you

_____ 12. money that is given back to you if you are not happy with something you paid for

Abbreviations

Match the abbreviation with the word or words that it represents.

When we write about stores and shopping, we often use abbreviations. When you read an abbreviation, you say the whole word. For example, when you read *dept.* you say *department.*

_____ 1. dept.   a. assistant

_____ 2. mgr.   b. incorporated

_____ 3. asst.   c. paid

_____ 4. co.   d. department

_____ 5. Inc.   e. company

_____ 6. misc.   f. miscellaneous

_____ 7. pd.   g. package

_____ 8. pkg.   h. manager

Compound Words

Choose a word from each box. Combine the words into a compound word and write the new word on the line.

Compound words are words made up of two or more words. Each is written as one word and has a special meaning that comes from the combination of words.

book	high	passage	up
down	in	side	wheel

chairs	stairs	town	way
doors	store	walk	ways

1. She hates malls and shopping centers, so she shops _____.

2. She bought a book and a magazine at the _____.

3. The mall has two levels. Her favorite stores are _____.

4. The shopping center is near the _____, so it is easy to get there by car.

5. Since the mall is _____, you don't need a raincoat to go shopping on a rainy day.

6. The mall has wide _____ with benches where you can rest.

7. The mall has several elevators for customers who use _____.

8. There is a wide _____ in front of the stores in the shopping center.

Prefix

The prefix *semi–* can mean *half, partly,* or *happening twice in a period.*

Choose a word from the box, add *semi–* to it, and write it on the line.

annual	**conscious**	**final**	**sweet**
circle	**darkness**	**private**	

1. We get discounts twice a year when the stores have their _____ sales.

2. When the electricity went out, she couldn't see anything in the _____ of the passageways at the mall.

3. The man was _____ when they brought him into the hospital, but he was awake later.

4. At the hospital, they put the man in a _____ room which he had to share with one other person.

5. I stopped in a candy shop and bought some _____ chocolate.

6. They arranged the dresses in a _____ in the display at the shop.

7. In the tournament, the winners of the _____ games will play each other.

Suffix

The suffix *–ment* is used to change a verb into a noun.

Choose a verb from the box, add *–ment* to it, and write it on the line.

advertise	**employ**	**manage**	**ship**
agree	**entertain**	**pay**	

1. There is an _____ for that sale in today's newspaper.

2. Her credit card _____ is due on the 15th of the month.

3. The mall has a _____ office that is in charge of special events.

4. If you are looking for _____, the mall has six movie theaters.

5. Mary and Laura were in _____. They both hated the dress.

6. If you are looking for a job, go to the mall _____ office.

7. The department store is getting a new _____ of dresses next week.

Synonyms

Choose a word from the box which has about the same meaning as each underlined word or phrase. Write the word on the line.

advertised	buy	customer	purchase
assistance	credit	discount	work

1. That store values its <u>shoppers</u>. They say, "The _____ is always right."

2. They offered a 20% _____ and other <u>reduced</u> prices.

3. They _____ the discounts and <u>announced</u> another special sale.

4. I only <u>shop</u> at the mall. I never _____ anything downtown.

5. He's out of _____ and looking for <u>employment</u> at the mall.

6. I needed _____ in the fitting room, but I didn't get the <u>help</u> I needed.

7. I <u>charged</u> the dress on my _____ card.

8. I'm not going to _____ another dress, since I just <u>bought</u> this one.

Collocations

We use many two-word collocations when we talk about places where we shop.

Choose a word from the box and write it on the line.

counter	display	fitting	service
department	dress	lot	shopping

1. There's a big parking _____ in front of the shopping center.

2. I took three dresses into the _____ room.

3. There's a new discount _____ shop in the shopping center.

4. That _____ store has everything from socks to pots.

5. If you need to exchange that, go to customer _____.

6. You can park right in front of the store at the _____ center.

7. I took the items that I decided to buy to the check-out _____.

8. We looked at the watches in the _____ case.

Exercise 8

Confusing Words

Study the meaning of each combination and then write the correct word on the line.

When we talk about shopping, we use common verbs like *pick, take, try,* and *wait.* We change the meaning of the verbs by combining them with words like *back, for, off, on, out,* and *up.*

pick <u>out</u> means *choose* or *select*
pick <u>up</u> means *to lift something from a surface or to buy something while you are going somewhere*
take <u>back</u> means *to return an item that you bought*
take <u>off</u> means *to remove something, especially a piece of clothing*
try <u>on</u> means *to put a piece of clothing on to see if it is the right size and/or if it looks good on you*
try <u>out</u> means *to test something such as a piece of equipment to see if it works well*
wait <u>for</u> means *to delay doing something until something else happens*
wait <u>on</u> means *to assist someone in a shop or store*

1. While I was at the mall, I picked _____ a package of socks.

2. I took the shoes _____ immediately because they were too small.

3. I liked the salesperson who waited _____ me.

4. If you are going to the drugstore, could you pick _____ some toothpaste?

5. Before you buy that jacket, you should try it _____.

6. After I bought the dress, I needed to pick _____ some new shoes.

7. I'm going to take this sweater _____ because it has a hole in it.

8. I'll wait _____ you on a bench in the mall.

9. I'm not going to buy that hair dryer unless I can try it _____ first.

10. The pants fit, so I have to pick _____ a shirt that matches.

11. I needed help, but there was no one to wait _____ me.

12. If you want to see how heavy it is, you have to pick it _____.

13. The hair dryer doesn't work. Let's take it _____.

14. The salesperson had to pick _____ the clothes that fell on the floor.

15. It's warm and dry in the mall, so you can take your coat _____.

16. I wanted to try _____ that new CD player before I bought it.

Context Clues

Choose a word or phrase from below
each line and write it on the line.

> It is often possible to guess a missing word from the context of a sentence. When you rely on context, you use what you know about the other words in the sentence to help you guess the word.

1. She likes to shop _____ because it doesn't matter what the
   downtown / at the shopping center / at the mall
   weather is. It can be hot, cold, or rainy outside, and she is always comfortable shopping.

2. She cut a _____ out of the newspaper. If she uses it when she
   coupon / advertisement / payment
   buys something, she will save 20%.

3. I took four pairs of jeans into the _____, but I didn't like any
   customer service / check-out counter / fitting room
   of them.

4. He is looking for a job and would like to work at the mall. Last week, he went to pick up an
   application at the _____ office there.
   entertainment / employment / department

5. If you want to buy something at a discount, you have to wait for the
   _____ sale, which only happens twice a year.
   semiannual / semiweekly / semiprivate

6. If you just bought that coat and it doesn't fit, I think you should take it
   _____.
   off / back / on

7. I don't want to exchange this for another coat. I just want a _____.
   refund / discount / return
   Since I paid cash, it should be easy to get my money back.

8. There aren't any watches in the display case at the department store. When I asked about
   that, the clerk told me that a new _____ is going to arrive
   agreement / payment / shipment
   tomorrow, so they will have a lot of watches then.

Parts of Speech

Identify the underlined words. Write *N* on the line if the word is a noun, and write *V* if it is a verb.

> Many common vocabulary words that end in *–s* can work either as plural nouns or as third-person singular verbs. Look for a noun after a verb, and look for a verb after a subject (a person or a place).

_____ 1. That discount store doesn't give <u>refunds</u>, but you can exchange items.

_____ 2. My friend <u>purchases</u> a lot of items and then returns half of them.

_____ 3. That store <u>discounts</u> all of its merchandise in the semiannual sale.

_____ 4. Every morning the clerks straighten <u>displays</u> and organize merchandise.

_____ 5. The store manager <u>refunds</u> your money if you are not happy with your purchase.

_____ 6. The sign said, "Take <u>purchases</u> to the check-out counter."

_____ 7. I shop at that store because they offer <u>discounts</u> on everything.

_____ 8. The jewelry store <u>displays</u> the watches in glass cases.

Dictionary

Identify the part of speech of each underlined word. Write *N* or *V* on the line. Then look up the word in your dictionary. Choose and write the best definition.

_____ 1. My classmate and I <u>exchanged</u> phone numbers, but I don't think I will call her.

definition: _____

_____ 2. You can use my dictionary as long as you <u>return</u> it right away.

definition: _____

_____ 3. You can buy the watches, but the display case is not for <u>sale</u>.

definition: _____

_____ 4. My car is in the <u>shop</u>, so I'll take the bus to the mall.

definition: _____

_____ 5. The coupon is good on <u>purchases</u> of more than $50.

definition: _____

Crossword Puzzle

Fill in the puzzle with words from the box.

back	customer	display	fitting	passageways	semicircle	service
co.	dept.	employment	Mgr.	payment	semidarkness	
coupon	discount	exchange	out	refund	semiweekly	

ACROSS

1. The abbreviation for *department* is _____.
4. The manager says, "The _____ is always right."
6. If you need to exchange that, go to customer _____.
8. I'm going to exchange this coat so I need to pick _____ another one.
10. I looked at the watches in the _____ case.
12. If you have a credit card, you usually have to make a _____ every month.
13. If you see _____ in a store's name, it means *company*.
15. _____ is the abbreviation for *manager*.
16. If you need a job, you can fill out an _____ application.
17. If you want your money back, ask for a _____.
18. If it is twice a week, then it is _____.

DOWN

1. That _____ store has lower prices on everything.
2. I couldn't see in the _____ after the electricity went out.
3. The mall has covered _____ with benches where people can rest.
5. I cut a _____ out of the newspaper.
7. A _____ is half of a circle.
9. I decided to take the dress _____ since I didn't like it.
11. Take the jeans into the _____ room to try them on.
14. If you don't like it, you can _____ it or get a refund.

Vocabulary in Context

Choose a word from the box and write it on the line.

advertisement	department	mall	shipment
coupon	discount	semiannual	

I saw an _____ in the newspaper for a _____ sale at the
1   2

_____ store. Since I need a new watch, I cut out the _____
3   4

and went to the _____. The store had just gotten a big _____
5   6

of watches, and I bought one at a 45% _____.
7

assist	center	fitting	highway	picked	shop

I had a terrible shopping trip last weekend. I needed a dress for graduation, so I went to the

discount dress _____ in the shopping _____ near the
8   9

_____. I _____ out three dresses and took them into the
10   11

_____ room. The room was filled with clothes and was very messy. There was
12

no one available to _____ me, either.
13

for	on	on	off	out	up

Last week my watch broke, so I decided to buy a new one. I went to the jewelry department in

the department store to pick _____ a new one. I saw a gold watch, but when I
14

picked it _____, it was too heavy, so I didn't like it. Then I found a silver one. I
15

tried it _____ and I liked it, but the band was too big. I took it
16

_____, and the clerk who was waiting _____ me said they
17   18

could shorten the band. Now I am waiting _____ a call from the store telling
19

me my watch is ready.

Answer Key

Lesson 1, pp. 8-17

Exercise 1, p. 9
1. noun	5. consonant	9. stress
2. compound word	6. vowel	10. verb
3. plural	7. pronoun	11. adjective
4. adverb	8. intonation	12. collocation

Exercise 2, p. 10
1. e 2. c 3. h 4. a 5. f 6. b 7. d 8. g

Exercise 3, p. 10
1. daytime	3. classmates	5. bookshelf	7. textbook
2. himself	4. themselves	6. weekend	8. without

Exercise 4, p. 11
1. biweekly	3. bicycle	5. biplane
2. bilingual	4. bimonthly	6. bicentennial

Exercise 5, p. 11
1. acceptable	4. comfortable	7. disagreeable
2. countable	5. breakable	8. predictable
3. enjoyable	6. dependable	

Exercise 6, p. 12
1. grammar	3. vocabulary	5. improve	7. oral
2. syntax	4. idioms	6. courses	8. difficulty

Exercise 7, p. 12
1. pie 2. pin 3. rock 4. hills 5. gold 6. bear

Exercise 8, p. 13
1. for	5. since	9. a little	13. a little
2. since	6. since	10. a few	14. a little
3. for	7. for	11. a few	15. a few
4. for	8. since	12. a few	16. a few

Exercise 9, p. 14
1. singular	3. adjective	5. stress	7. syntax
2. vocabulary	4. punctuation	6. articles	8. pronouns

Exercise 10, p. 15
1. N 2. N 3. V 4. V 5. N 6. V 7. N 8. V

Exercise 11, p. 15
Definitions will vary.
1. N 2. N 3. N 4. V 5. N

Review 1, p. 16

Across
4. collocation	9. countable	14. syntax
6. prep.	12. oral	16. difficulty
7. bimonthly	13. pie	18. vowel

Down
1. plural	5. art.	11. weekend
2. compound	8. little	15. rock
3. bilingual	10. bookshelf	17. few

Review 2, p. 17
1. trouble	6. bicycle	11. classmates
2. consonant	7. daytime	12. textbook
3. vowel	8. dependable	13. without
4. stress	9. biweekly	14. himself
5. intonation	10. enjoyable	15. idioms

Lesson 2, pp. 18-27

Exercise 1, p. 19
1. documentary	4. commercial	7. antenna	10. sitcom
2. broadcast	5. drama	8. inform	11. local
3. soap opera	6. entertain	9. live	12. cable

Exercise 2, p. 20
1. d 2. f 3. a 4. h 5. e 6. c 7. g 8. b

Exercise 3, p. 20
1. baseball	3. earthquake	5. weekdays	7. housework
2. weatherman	4. updates	6. eyewitness	8. newspapers

Exercise 4, p. 21
1. telescope	3. telephone	5. television
2. telecommunications	4. telephoto	6. telegraph

Exercise 5, p. 21
1. televise	3. exercise	5. surprise	7. supervise
2. advertise	4. improvise	6. compromise	8. despise

Exercise 6, p. 22
1. dramas	3. live	5. daytime	7. local
2. funny	4. boring	6. love	8. serious

Exercise 7, p. 22
1. up 2. into 3. down 4. on 5. off 6. up

Exercise 8, p. 23
1. watch	5. watch	9. likes	13. like
2. see	6. watch	10. likes	14. would like
3. watch	7. see	11. would like	15. likes
4. see	8. watches	12. would like	16. likes

Exercise 9, p. 24
1. advertise	3. weather	5. antenna	7. improvise
2. documentary	4. weekday	6. reporters	8. informative

Exercise 10, p. 25
1. N 2. V 3. V 4. V 5. N 6. V 7. N 8. N

Exercise 11, p. 25
Definitions will vary.
1. N 2. N 3. V 4. N 5. N

Review 1, p. 26

Across
1. watched	7. taped	13. surprise	16. housework
3. sitcoms	9. comedies	14. NBC	
4. live	11. telescope	15. commercials	

Down
2. compromise	6. updates	10. MTV
5. eyewitnesses	8. documentary	12. CNN

Review 2, p. 27
1. entertains	5. cable	9. down	13. televise
2. informs	6. into	10. off	14. compromise
3. broadcast	7. on	11. despise	15. supervise
4. antenna	8. up	12. advertise	

Lesson 3, pp. 28-37

Exercise 1, p. 29
1. respond	4. greeting	7. fold	10. postage
2. deliver	5. envelope	8. closing	11. address
3. sign	6. compose	9. body	12. return address

Exercise 2, p. 30

1. e   2. a   3. f   4. h   5. g   6. b   7. d   8. c

Exercise 3, p. 30

1. something   3. handwriting   5. grandfather   7. wastebasket
2. birthday   4. deadline   6. notebook   8. postcard

Exercise 4, p. 31

1. postscript   3. posttest   5. postoperative   7. postwar
2. postsecondary   4. postgame   6. postseason   8. postdate

Exercise 5, p. 31

1. formal   3. comical   5. professional   7. emotional
2. personal   4. central   6. national   8. optional

Exercise 6, p. 32

1. compose   3. sincerely   5. formal   7. stamp
2. salutation   4. personal   6. response

Exercise 7, p. 32

1. post   3. first-class   5. return   7. box
2. Code   4. apartment   6. address

Exercise 8, p. 33

1. right   5. write   9. bend   13. bent
2. right   6. right   10. fold   14. folded
3. write   7. right   11. folded   15. bend
4. write   8. write   12. bend   16. folded

Exercise 9, p. 34

1. Zip Code   3. signature   5. deliver   7. postcard
2. dear   4. business   6. envelope   8. respond

Exercise 10, p. 35

1. Adj.   3. Adv.   5. Adv.   7. Adj.
2. Adv.   4. Adj.   6. Adj.   8. Adv.

Exercise 11, p. 35

Definitions will vary.
1. V   2. V   3. N   4. V   5. V

Review 1, p. 36

Across

6. postscript   9. envelope   12. folded   16. TX
7. body   11. AZ   15. sincerely   17. carrier

Down

1. respond   4. stationery   8. deadline   14. compose
2. wastebasket   5. postage   10. VA
3. ZIP   6. professional   13. personal

Review 2, p. 37

1. greeting   5. signed   9. carriers   13. postage   17. VA
2. body   6. folded   10. box   14. TX   18. CO
3. compose   7. envelope   11. Code   15. PA
4. sincerely   8. office   12. change   16. AZ

Lesson 4, pp. 38-47

Exercise 1, p. 39

1. detector   4. buckle   7. agent   10. board
2. pass   5. reach   8. checkpoint   11. proceed
3. terminal   6. check   9. hassle   12. luggage

Exercise 2, p. 40

1. d   2. a   3. f   4. e   5. c   6. b

Exercise 3, p. 40

1. passport   3. backpack   5. cabdriver   7. goodbye
2. thunderstorm   4. skyscrapers   6. walkways   8. aircraft

Exercise 4, p. 41

1. uniforms   3. unique   5. unicycle
2. universal   4. unite   6. union

Exercise 5, p. 41

1. attendants   3. assistant   5. contestant   7. accountant
2. occupants   4. inhabitants   6. servants   8. immigrant

Exercise 6, p. 42

1. baggage   3. fastened   5. aircraft   7. departed
2. arrived   4. traveler   6. restroom   8. pilot

Exercise 7, p. 42

1. on   3. off   5. out   7. off
2. up   4. in   6. off   8. at

Exercise 8, p. 43

1. rides or rode   6. riding   11. flies or flew   16. rides or rode
2. flies or flew   7. sails   12. drive   17. fly
3. ride   8. fly   13. sail or sailed   18. drove
4. sailed   9. ride   14. ride   19. ride
5. drives or drove   10. drive   15. fly   20. fly

Exercise 9, p. 44

1. passengers   3. luggage   5. lavatory   7. check
2. ticket agent   4. checkpoint   6. fly   8. reaches

Exercise 10, p. 45

1. V   3. V   5. Adj.   7. Adj.
2. Adj.   4. V   6. V   8. Adj.

Exercise 11, p. 45

Definitions will vary.
1. V   2. V   3. N   4. V   5. N

Review 1, p. 46

Across

2. terminal   8. landed   13. passport   17. FAA
3. up   9. TSA   14. off   18. detector
5. luggage   12. assistant   16. uniforms

Down

1. buckle   4. attendants   7. lavatory   11. walkway
2. thunderstorm   6. checkpoint   10. DHS   15. board

Review 2, p. 47

1. hassle   5. boarded   9. flew   13. departed
2. terminal   6. backpack   10. drove   14. pilot
3. checkpoint   7. fastened   11. rode   15. taken off
4. gate   8. took   12. sailed   16. landed

Lesson 5, pp. 48-57

Exercise 1, p. 49

1. chef   5. waitress / waiter   9. busboy
2. apron   6. entrée   10. menu
3. reservation   7. appetizer   11. server
4. seat   8. hostess / host   12. beverage

Exercise 2, p. 50

1. b   2. h   3. c   4. e   5. f   6. g   7. d   8. a

Exercise 3, p. 50

1. restroom   3. dishwashers   5. teacups   7. cheeseburger
2. busboy   4. tablecloths   6. blackboard   8. indoors

Exercise 4, p. 51

1. undercharged   4. underweight   7. underpaid
2. underused   5. underestimated   8. undersized
3. undercooked   6. underrated

Exercise 5, p. 51

1. actress   3. heiress   5. stewardesses   7. hostess
2. waitress   4. princess   6. goddesses

Exercise 6, p. 52

1. entrance   3. served   5. alcohol   7. entrées
2. chef   4. ordered   6. beverage   8. restrooms

Exercise 7, p. 52

1. shakers	3. area	5. dishes	7. order
2. on	4. dining	6. counter	

Exercise 8, p. 53

1. for	4. for	7. for	10. wait	13. weight	16. wait
2. on	5. for	8. on	11. weight	14. weight	
3. on	6. on	9. wait	12. wait	15. wait	

Exercise 9, p. 54

1. menu	3. restroom	5. seated	7. appetizer
2. chef	4. dishwasher	6. order	8. undercharged

Exercise 10, p. 55

1. N   2. V   3. N   4. V   5. N   6. N   7. V   8. V

Exercise 11, p. 55

Definitions will vary.
1. V   2. N   3. N   4. N   5. V

Review 1, p. 56

Across

2. blackboard	10. busboy	13. hostess	17. entrance
4. out	11. beverage	14. Tsp.	
9. actresses	12. waitress	15. appetizers	

Down

1. underrated	5. underestimated	7. reservation	16. Gal.
3. liquor	6. dishwasher	8. Lb.	

Review 2, p. 57

1. hostesses	5. servers	9. pt.	13. undersized
2. waitresses	6. busboys	10. qt.	14. undercooked
3. chef	7. tsp.	11. lb.	15. underpaid
4. cooks	8. tbsp.	12. oz.	16. undercharged

Lesson 6, pp. 58-67

Exercise 1, p. 59

1. produce	4. bakery	7. groceries	10. aisle
2. stock	5. convenient	8. package	11. selection
3. cart	6. shelf	9. deli	12. brand

Exercise 2, p. 60

1. b   2. h   3. g   4. d   5. c   6. f   7. a   8. e

Exercise 3, p. 60

1. cardboard	3. blueberries	5. everything	7. drugstore
2. toothpaste	4. nearby	6. seafood	8. homemade

Exercise 4, p. 61

1. superstar	4. superpowers	7. superman
2. supercomputer	5. superheroes	8. supermarket
3. supermodel	6. superhuman	

Exercise 5, p. 61

1. cheaper	3. larger	5. nicer	7. fresher
2. newer	4. cleaner	6. neater	8. faster

Exercise 6, p. 62

1. fresh	3. old-fashioned	5. dirty	7. empty
2. expensive	4. enormous	6. speedy	8. polite

Exercise 7, p. 62

1. aisle	3. name	5. coupon	7. register
2. manager	4. card	6. lot	8. carts

Exercise 8, p. 63

1. ad	6. pears	11. by	16. meat	21. ate
2. hire	7. aisle	12. their	17. cereal	22. pair
3. eight	8. sale	13. hole	18. there	
4. cent	9. serial	14. higher	19. sent	
5. whole	10. meet	15. add	20. flour	

Exercise 9, p. 64

1. brand	3. cart	5. shelf	7. selection
2. convenient	4. deli	6. blueberries	8. seafood

Exercise 10, p. 65

1. V   2. N   3. N   4. V   5. N   6. V   7. V   8. N

Exercise 11, p. 65

Definitions will vary.
1. Adj.   2. V   3. N   4. V   5. V

Review 1, p. 66

Across

2. shelves	8. cardboard	11. Ea.	16. Dept.
3. stocks	9. aisle	12. selection	
7. modern	10. Pkg.	15. blueberries	

Down

1. homemade	4. shopping	6. enormous	13. brand
2. supermarket	5. groceries	10. produce	14. deli

Review 2, p. 67

1. clean	6. modern	11. seafood	16. shelf
2. tiny	7. convenient	12. parking	17. aisle
3. empty	8. nearby	13. bakery	18. register
4. fresh	9. everything	14. produce	
5. speedy	10. drugstore	15. deli	

Lesson 7, pp. 68-77

Exercise 1, p. 69

1. damp	4. blizzard	7. hurricane	10. chilly
2. climate	5. thunderstorm	8. tornado	11. severe
3. hail	6. frost	9. forecast	12. mild

Exercise 2, p. 70

1. h   2. e   3. b   4. f   5. g   6. d   7. a   8. c

Exercise 3, p. 70

1. weatherman	3. northwest	5. snowball	7. driveway
2. thunderstorm	4. sunshine	6. raindrops	8. daylight

Exercise 4, p. 71

1. before	3. front	5. before	7. before
2. front	4. before	6. front	8. before

Exercise 5, p. 71

1. rainiest	3. hottest	5. driest	7. chilliest
2. sunniest	4. wettest	6. windiest	8. earliest

Exercise 6, p. 72

1. cloudy	3. warm	5. windy	7. earlier
2. humid	4. freezes	6. rises	8. lightly

Exercise 7, p. 72

1. thunder	3. night	5. dense	7. hot
2. rain	4. partly	6. sleet	

Exercise 8, p. 73

1. a few	5. a little	9. too many	13. too many
2. a little	6. a little	10. too much	14. too much
3. a few	7. a little	11. too much	15. too many
4. a few	8. a few	12. too many	16. too many

Exercise 9, p.74

1. sunshine	3. severe	5. blizzard	7. frost
2. chilly	4. thaw	6. Hail	8. windy

Exercise 10, p. 75

1. Adv.	3. Adj.	5. Adj.	7. Adv.
2. Adv.	4. Adv.	6. Adj.	8. adj.

Exercise 11, p. 75

Definitions will vary.
1. Adj.   2. Adv.   3. V   4. Adj.   5. V

Review 1, p. 76

Across

1. rainiest   7. humid   13. windiest   17. earliest
6. snowman   8. weatherman   16. avg.   18. partly

Down

2. straight   5. sunshine   11. rises   15. hail
3. forecast   9. foresee   12. thaw
4. forewarned   10. blizzard   14. temp.

Review 2, p. 77

1. climate   6. hard   11. northwest   16. temp.
2. damp   7. mild   12. raindrops   17. avg.
3. severe   8. thunderstorm   13. driveway   18. F
4. tornado   9. humid   14. lightning   19. UV
5. frost   10. partly   15. hail   20. max.

Lesson 8, pp. 78-87

Exercise 1, p. 79

1. training   5. experience   9. skill
2. certificate   6. mechanic   10. aide
3. receptionist   7. qualification   11. diploma
4. announcement   8. search   12. application

Exercise 2, p. 80

1. d   2. c   3. h   4. a   5. g   6. b   7. e   8. f

Exercise 3, p. 80

1. policeman   3. housekeeper   5. firefighter   7. hairdresser
2. salesperson   4. dishwasher   6. lifeguard   8. bartender

Exercise 4, p. 81

1. outsell   3. outlive   5. outnumber   7. outrun
2. outranks   4. outweigh   6. outbid   8. outshine

Exercise 5, p. 81

1. assistant   3. accountant   5. applicants   7. contestant
2. consultant   4. attendant   6. servant

Exercise 6, p. 82

1. assists   3. supervisor   5. assistant   7. employee
2. mall   4. factory   6. training   8. experience

Exercise 7, p. 82

1. teller   3. carrier   5. officer   7. guard
2. aide   4. driver   6. server   8. processor

Exercise 8, p. 83

1. advise   7. advice   13. advice
2. advice   8. advise   14. recommendations
3. advice   9. recommendations   15. advice
4. advise   10. advice   16. advice
5. advice   11. recommendations   17. recommendations
6. advise   12. recommendations   18. Recommendations

Exercise 9, p. 84

1. announcements   4. bartender   7. nurse's aide
2. experience   5. outnumber   8. certificate
3. qualifications   6. dishwasher

Exercise 10, p. 85

1. Adj.   3. Adj.   5. V   7. V
2. V   4. Adj.   6. Adj.   8. V

Exercise 11, p. 85

Definitions will vary.
1. V   2. N   3. V   4. Adj.   5. V

Review 1, p. 86

Across

3. contestant   8. PT   12. lifeguards   15. teller
4. supervisor   11. factory   14. EOE   17. aide

Down

1. consultant   5. outweigh   9. hairdresser   16. ASAP
2. diploma   6. guard   10. FT
3. certificate   7. outsells   13. search

Review 2, p. 87

1. certificate   6. skills   11. housekeeper   16. driver
2. application   7. bartender   12. carrier   17. guard
3. mechanic   8. salesperson   13. officer
4. experience   9. firefighter   14. firefighter
5. training   10. lifeguard   15. training

Lesson 9, pp. 88-97

Exercise 1, p. 89

1. root for   4. hiking   7. position   10. professional
2. catcher   5. pitcher   8. rink   11. goalie
3. fan   6. tournament   9. court   12. touchdown

Exercise 2, p. 90

1. g   2. h   3. e   4. a   5. f   6. d   7. c   8. b

Exercise 3, p. 90

1. hometown   3. basketball   5. shortstop   7. goalkeeper
2. touchdown   4. quarterback   6. roommates   8. outfield

Exercise 4, p. 91

1. 1   2. 3   3. 2   4. 2   5. 3   6. 2   7. 1   8. 3

Exercise 5, p. 91

1. shopping   3. skating   5. running   7. biking
2. riding   4. jogging   6. hiking   8. swimming

Exercise 6, p. 92

1. exciting   3. amateur   5. artificial   7. hits
2. burning   4. national   6. freezes

Exercise 7, p. 92

1. baseball   3. soccer   5. ski   7. hiking
2. tennis   4. hockey   6. swimming

Exercise 8, p. 93

1. their   5. They're   9. There   13. They're   17. there
2. there   6. their   10. There   14. they're   18. their
3. They're   7. there   11. their   15. They're   19. They're
4. There   8. They're   12. their   16. there   20. there

Exercise 9, p. 94

1. football   3. basketball   5. swimming   7. ball
2. soccer   4. baseball   6. skating   8. uniforms

Exercise 10, p. 95

1. N   2. N   3. V   4. V   5. N   6. V   7. V   8. N

Exercise 11, p. 95

Definitions will vary.
1. N   2. V   3. V   4. N   5. V

Review 1, p. 96

Across

1. root for   11. their   15. score   19. PGA
4. stadium   12. hometown   16. rink
8. catcher   14. ESPN   17. tournament

Down

2. triathlon   6. diamond   10. uniforms
3. quarterback   7. There   13. goalie
5. touchdown   9. professional   18. NFL

Review 2, p. 97

1. position	6. hiking	11. biking	16. NHL
2. shortstop	7. skating	12. riding	17. NCAA
3. court	8. swimming	13. ESPN	
4. goalkeeper	9. running	14. NBA / WNBA	
5. quarterback	10. jogging	15. WNBA / NBA	

Lesson 10, pp. 98-107

Exercise 1, p. 99

1. fitting room	5. exchange	9. shopping center
2. mall	6. advertisement	10. coupon
3. customer service	7. return	11. try on
4. discount	8. downtown	12. refund

Exercise 2, p. 100

1. d   2. h   3. a   4. e   5. b   6. f   7. c   8. g

Exercise 3, p. 100

1. downtown	3. upstairs	5. indoors	7. wheelchairs
2. bookstore	4. highway	6. passageways	8. sidewalk

Exercise 4, p. 101

1. semiannual	4. semiprivate	7. semifinal
2. semidarkness	5. semisweet	
3. semiconscious	6. semicircle	

Exercise 5, p. 101

1. advertisement	4. entertainment	7. shipment
2. payment	5. agreement	
3. management	6. employment	

Exercise 6, p. 102

1. customer	3. advertised	5. work	7. credit
2. discount	4. buy	6. assistance	8. purchase

Exercise 7, p. 102

1. lot	3. dress	5. service	7. counter
2. fitting	4. department	6. shopping	8. display

Exercise 8, p. 103

1. up	4. up	7. off	10. out	13. back	16. out
2. off	5. on	8. for	11. on	14. up	
3. on	6. out	9. out	12. up	15. off	

Exercise 9, p. 104

1. at the mall	3. fitting room	5. semiannual	7. refund
2. coupon	4. employment	6. back	8. shipment

Exercise 10, p. 105

1. N   2. V   3. V   4. N   5. V   6. N   7. N   8. V

Exercise 11, p. 105

Definitions will vary.
1. V   2. V   3. N   4. N   5. N

Review 1, p. 106

Across

1. dept.	8. out	13. co.	17. refund
4. customer	10. display	15. Mgr.	18. semiweekly
6. service	12. payment	16. employment	

Down

1. discount	3. passageways	7. semicircle	11. fitting
2. semidarkness	5. coupon	9. back	14. exchange

Review 2, p. 107

1. advertisement	6. shipment	11. picked	16. on
2. semiannual	7. discount	12. fitting	17. off
3. department	8. shop	13. assist	18. on
4. coupon	9. center	14. out	19. for
5. mall	10. highway	15. up	